Praise for *The Hidden Mec*

Kate Wilson's 'The Hidden Mechanics of IP' is simply a delightful read, providing step-by-step guidance for entrepreneurs of all stripes to use in advancing their businesses. Every business person should read this book to reveal and unlock business opportunity so many fail to fully appreciate or completely overlook.

— DAVID KAPPOS

Former USPTO Director and current partner at
NYC law firm Cravath, Swaine & Moore L.L.P

It is by far the best book of its type I have come across. Kate has done an absolutely brilliant job. She gets IP and she gets business but, most important, she gets that her audience needs to be engaged immediately and that it wants practical, grounded insight and advice.

— JOFF WILD

Founder and former editor-in-chief of
IAM - Intellectual Asset Magazine (2003 to 2022)

Real-world examples illustrate what, and what not, to do and provide concrete, valuable lessons in navigating potential opportunities and hazards.

— MICHELLE HOULE

Publications editor for the Battersby Law Group
and WK Licensing Journal

Invaluable to marketers everywhere, to corporates, to financial types, to start-ups, to founders, to entrepreneurs, to designers, to creatives, to chief executives, and yes – even to lawyers.

— KEVIN ROBERTS

Former Chairman and CEO,
Saatchi & Saatchi Worldwide Founder, Red Rose Consulting

This is a business strategy manual disguised as an IP Guide. Read it before you start your next project or set your next strategy.

— DR. LEE MATHIAS OMNZ

A valuable read for any founder looking to raise capital, stand out from the competition, and scale with confidence.

— ANNA DEVCICH
General Manager, Soda Inc.

Fantastic resource for anyone wanting to understand and monetise IP.

— TONY KANE
Business Advisor Phae Group Ltd

Having been involved in dozens of IP or Trademark related exercises throughout my career I can only lament this book not having been around before! It provides an outstanding contribution to the demystification of the arcane craft of IP otherwise known and understood by few practitioners.

— MIKE HUTCHESON M.PHIL.(1ST CLASS HONS) FCIM.
Company Director, Writer, Former CEO,
Saatchi & Saatchi and Adjunct Professor AUT

Kate's Three Cogs concept will continue to provide excellent value for investors and startups alike in this very digestible book.

— WARREN BEBB
Chief Investment Officer - Sprout Agritech

KATE WILSON

THE HIDDEN MECHANICS OF IP™

DEMYSTIFYING INTELLECTUAL PROPERTY

iX

indieXperts

PUBLISHING & AUTHOR SERVICES

First Published 2025

Published by Kate Wilson

Produced by Indie Experts
www.indieexpertspublishing.com

Copyright © Kate Wilson 2025

The moral right of the author to be identified as the author of this work has been asserted.

All rights reserved. Except for the purposes of reviewing, no part of this publication may be reproduced or transmitted in any form or by any means, electronic or mechanical, including photocopying, recording or any information storage or retrieval system, without the written permission of the author. Infringers of copyright render themselves liable for prosecution.

Cover design and typesetting by
Ammie Christiansen, Fast Forward Design
Typeset in 11pt Minion Pro

ISBN:
978-1-0670933-0-3 (Hardcover)
978-1-0670933-2-7 (Printed)
978-1-0670933-1-0 (eBook)

Disclaimer:
Every effort has been made to ensure this book is as accurate and complete as possible, however they may be errors both typographical and in content. The author and the publisher shall not be held liable or responsible to any person or entity with respect to any loss or damage caused or alleged to have been caused directly or indirectly by the information contained in this book.

Some names and identifying details in this book have been changed to protect the privacy of individuals.

FOREWORD

It was 20 years ago today (thank you John and Paul) that I came to know a funky, fearless, foodie-loving Kiwi patent attorney called Kate (yes – an oxymoron – a funky attorney!!).

A Science graduate with a passion – of all things – for Intellectual Property.

She single-handedly reframed I.P. for me from a dull, technical chore to an integral tool in creating and developing Brands and Lovemarks, protecting them and ensuring they could breathe and grow freely – and profitably!

She has finally come to her senses and decided to share her knowledge, experience, insight and advice in a book – something we talked about many times – and here it is in all its glory.

The content is priceless.

Invaluable to marketers everywhere, to corporates, to financial types, to start-ups, to founders, to entrepreneurs, to designers, to creatives, to chief executives, and yes – even to lawyers.

The book is beautifully designed, funky, fun and easy on the eye. Don't take my word for it. Dip into any page and see for yourself.

It'll help you protect and grow your Brand and your Business.

Kevin Roberts

Former Chairman and CEO, Saatchi & Saatchi Worldwide
Founder, Red Rose Consulting

INTRODUCTION

*"I don't care that they stole my idea... I care
that they don't have any of their own."*

*NIKOLA TESLA, AN ELECTRIFYING SERBIAN-AMERICAN
ENGINEER, FUTURIST, AND INVENTOR*

The business landscape has undergone a profound transformation over
the past 50 years, driven by the forces of globalisation, the rise of the digital age, and the advent of instant communication. In the 1970s, physical assets such as land, buildings, machinery, and inventory accounted for 83% of a business's value. These assets were tangible, easily seen, and understood.

The value paradigm has shifted dramatically. Amazingly tangible assets now represent less than 10% of a business's total value. The lion's share—over 90%—is now held in intangible assets, or intellectual property (IP). Unlike physical assets, IP cannot be seen or touched. It encompasses ephemeral concepts such as know-how, innovations, culture, systems, brands, and designs.

Alarmingly, many businesses today remain unaware of the true importance of intellectual property. They fail to recognise that this critical component of their business can either multiply in value or be lost entirely, depending on how it is managed. Even more concerning is that many do not realise that intellectual property is a commercially viable asset that can be strategically leveraged to drive business growth.

To address this gap in understanding, I developed the **Hidden Mechanics**®—a framework designed to help businesses create, identify, capture, and commercialise their intellectual property. This approach has been central to my work in educating startups, established businesses, corporations, advisors, and investors alike. It also serves as the foundation for my approach to developing effective IP strategies.

This book will not only guide you through the application of the **Hidden Mechanics** but will also give you deeper insight into the world of intellectual property—and, I hope, unlock the true potential of your project or business.

DISCLAIMER

1) a renunciation of any claim to or connection with;
2) a disavowal
3) a statement made to save one's own ass.

From the Kevin Smith film, Dogma

DISCLAIMER

This book is intended to enhance your understanding of intellectual property issues in general and is not a substitute for professional advice tailored to your specific situation. For guidance on matters specific to your circumstances, please consult an IP specialist.

Keep in mind that IP law, its interpretation, and related business practices are continuously evolving. As a result, the content in this book may become outdated over time. Consider this a reason to look out for future editions.

Many images in this book are created primarily by me, either directly or supported by the creative use of generative AI. Publicly available images have been sourced from the likes of Patent Office records.

This is a highly personal book, reflecting my views and experiences. Other professionals may have different perspectives, and that's perfectly fine.

The stories and case studies included in this book are either:

✓ in the public domain; and/or
✓ shared with the permission of the parties involved; and/or
✓ sufficiently anonymised and modified to convey the message without revealing the source.

If you have any concerns or comments about the content, please feel free to reach out to me directly. I welcome your feedback and will consider making changes or improvements if needed. Compliments and endorsements are always appreciated!

CONTENTS

OVERVIEW
HIDDEN MECHANICS®

"I was happier when I was doing a mechanic's job."

HENRY FORD - AMERICAN INDUSTRIALIST AND BUSINESS MAGNATE

Intellectual property is by its nature invisible, yet it has a tangible effect being effectively the engine of a business – responsible for its success or otherwise…

Breaking down the analogy further, IP is the **Hidden Mechanics®** of a business. How IP is worked to ensure business success requires utilising three core principles – Competitive Edge, Competitive Intelligence and Collaboration. By imagining these principles as intermeshing cogs as part of the business mechanics, I finally had a way to conceptualise the role of intellectual property and explain how to use it successfully.

I designed the three cogs approach in **Hidden Mechanics** to be a straightforward yet powerful approach to maximising opportunities when launching a new project or revitalising a business. By understanding and applying just three key steps, you can significantly enhance your strategic positioning.

Competitive Edge

Imagine going on a treasure hunt, but instead of gold coins or jewels you uncover other hidden and somewhat unfathomable treasures. What are they worth? How do you secure them? And how do you get the most out of them?

In the business world, intellectual property is often the overlooked hidden treasure, and if unearthed, one that can be the catalyst that gives you an edge over your competitors.

The first cog in **Hidden Mechanics** is understanding intellectual property and its relevance in a business context.

From an IP perspective, competitive edge can be categorised into four key areas:

Brand – the most valuable IP; often encapsulated in trade mark registrations and supported by good systems

Operations and information – the backbone of any business; tricky to protect formally, relying upon relationships and good internal practices

Technological advances – cool inventions which are covered by patents and trade secrets and are sometimes open-sourced

Design – aesthetic creations whether in stylistic shape or patterns and afforded protection through copyright or design registrations.

This is by far the largest section of the book as it delves deeply into how to identify competitive edge. It also explores protection strategies, including patents, trade mark registrations, and business systems designed to capitalise on hidden assets.

The next cog of competitive intelligence arms businesses with guidance and focus that can help them optimise their competitive edge.

Competitive Intelligence

The cog of competitive Intelligence goes beyond standard market research and validation. It involves gathering comprehensive information about a competitive landscape using the lens of intellectual property.

This section discusses:
- ✓ IP searching
- ✓ assessing freedom to operate
- ✓ understanding competitors' IP
- ✓ identifying competitive tensions
- ✓ recognising barriers to entry that extend beyond formal IP protection.

With the market context of their competitive edges given by competitive intelligence, a business is now able to embark on world domination, whether under its own steam—or possibly faster, with collaborators.

The next cog of Collaboration gives tips on how to engage others to take your business further.

"Knowledge is Power"
– FRANCIS BACON, PHILOSOPHER AND FORMER
LORD CHANCELLOR OF ENGLAND

Collaboration

Collaboration is a concept that many entrepreneurial businesses find challenging to embrace, especially when scaling up. This includes identifying what you need, and from whom, to make your project a success.

Your project may need help in a number of areas which include:

✓ research

✓ manufacturing

✓ distribution

✓ brand associations

✓ complementary technologies.

The insights from Competitive Intelligence (the second **Cog**) will help you identify potential collaborators—remembering that even competitors can become collaborators. A well-protected Competitive Edge (the first **Cog**) can then be used as leverage in collaborator negotiations.

This section discusses deal-making strategies that can help businesses scale up effectively.

Three Cogs Summary

In essence, the Hidden Mechanics approach consists of:

1. using the first cog of Competitive Edge to understand what makes your innovation or project unique as well as how to capitalise upon that

2. using the second cog of Competitive Intelligence to provide market context

3. packaging the insights from the first two cogs to commercialise and capitalise upon your IP, whether independently or through the third cog of Collaboration.

I wish you the best in embarking upon the Hidden Mechanics journey. Good luck!

SECTION 1

THE 1ST COG
COMPETITIVE EDGE

"If you don't have a **COMPETITIVE** advantage, don't compete."
JACK WELCH, FORMER CHAIRMAN AND CEO OF GENERAL ELECTRIC

Competitive Edge – Overview

Jack Welch's stark quote cuts to the heart of business reality: to not just survive but thrive, a business must possess a clear competitive edge—something that sets it apart from the rest. Yet, many emerging businesses struggle to pinpoint what makes them truly special. Through diligent competitive intelligence and a critical self-assessment, business owners can uncover and articulate their unique strengths, often referred to as their Unique Selling Point (USP).

But having a USP isn't enough. It must translate into a tangible competitive advantage. This advantage could be operational, like efficient systems that reduce costs, consistently high-quality offerings, or a heightened responsiveness to customer needs. Alternatively, it could be external, offering customers (and investors) a compelling reason to choose your products or services over others.

Focusing on current and future revenue streams can help identify which aspects of a business provide a competitive edge. Often, the most profitable streams are linked to innovations within the product or the process of making it. In other cases, revenue might stem from brand value, where consumers are willing to pay a premium for a trusted name.

Surprisingly, even selling commodities or engaging in contract manufacturing—typically seen as competing on price—can be lucrative if backed by proactive strategies that leverage associated intellectual property.

Understanding these revenue streams (aka, it's all about the money) allows businesses to implement mechanisms that preserve and enhance their competitive edge.

The following section helps you identify **The Four Quarters** into which competitive edge falls, as well as the laws, systems, and strategies to make the best of each quarter. But first, let's explore what kind of thinking you need to work through as part of starting your IP journey.

Show me the money

Home printers are cheap and have loads of clever technical features, which is what compels consumers to buy them. These features are usually patented so the manufacturers can have a monopoly in the features that form their selling point.

Printers have been deliberately sold cheaply in order for the manufacturer to lock in a customer. This is because the main revenue stream comes not from the printer purchase but the consumables, such as ink cartridges.

By designing the ink cartridges so they can be the only ones that work with a particular printer, and protecting the associated IP, the original manufacturer effectively forces the consumer to purchase the cartridges from only them. Thus, the revenue stream from sale of the ink is secured.

Therefore, look at where the revenue streams can come from, innovate accordingly, and protect the associated IP.

1

IS IT WORTH IT?

"A cynic is a man who knows the price of
everything and the value of nothing."
OSCAR WILDE, IRISH POET AND PLAYWRIGHT

Frankly, paying for IP protection can be an enormous suck of money.

However, IP protection can also turn out to be one of the smartest investments a business ever makes. IP rights grant exclusive rights. They enable businesses to prevent others from manufacturing, selling, importing, or exporting whatever their IP rights cover.

Deciding whether to invest in IP depends on how clearly a business understands its future goals. Much of this clarity stems from the Competitive Intelligence a company gathers and its Competitive Edge—the first two Cogs of the Hidden Mechanics. **IP investment should always align with a company's ambitions, projected returns, and available resources.**

I love it when my clients' ambitions extend to world domination—and some even go as far as galactic domination with their inventions destined for space travel. While I can and do design IP strategies that cover these potential scenarios, often the strategies are tempered to account for achievable resources to implement them.

Expanding globally can be incredibly seductive at the beginning of an IP journey. Speaking with mentors and IP advisors about the value of protecting your IP in specific markets can help guide these decisions. Be realistic about whether the identified markets can deliver enough returns in a reasonable time frame to make the investment worthwhile. It's important to ensure there are still resources available to commercialise the business effectively.

To help clients make smart IP investment choices—whether for patents, design registrations, trade marks, or plant variety rights—I use a triaged approach, as outlined in the next chapter.

2

MARKET DECISIONS

"Business is war. I go out there, I want to kill the competitors. I want to make their lives miserable. I want to steal their market share. I want them to fear me and I want everyone on my team thinking we're going to win."

KEVIN O'LEARY, CANADIAN BUSINESSMAN AND SHARK TANK STALWART

Working through the following questions can guide your decision about where to invest in IP protection—noting that Competitive Intelligence research (discussed in Section 2) can provide some of the answers. Bear in mind that worldwide IP filings are usually neither affordable nor necessary for most businesses. Selecting the right countries is critical.

Where are you based?

Sadly, many competitors can emerge from among ex-employees and former business partners. So, always file in your home country. It can also help to have home-based IP protection when selling your business.

Where will you manufacture?

Invest in IP protection in your base of manufacture. If you are outsourcing manufacture, then terms related to IP protection can be included in the manufacturing agreement.

Where will competitors manufacture?

If a competitor has one or only a few manufacturing sites from which it exports, then a strategic move can be to block export at source by filing for IP protection where they manufacture—rather than where either you or they sell.

Where are you and your competitors currently selling or planning to sell?

Think carefully where you want a monopoly. Are you concerned if a competitor sells product in a market that you are not interested in? Or do you consider that they could be a collaborator and file where you think you can reasonably license your rights to them?

Where are potential third-party relationships, such as licensees or distributors, based?

If you are considering doing deals with third parties, then look at where they are based. Filing for rights in their countries/markets may help swing a deal.

What are the relative market sizes and how easy are they to navigate?

It is not enough to look at the numerical size of a suitable demographic in a market (TAM—Total Addressable Market). Accessibility to that demographic must also be considered (SAM—Serviceable Addressable Market)

Be aware that some routes to market can be difficult to navigate, particularly if there are regulatory barriers, such as those in the medical, veterinary and food industries or excessive tariffs.

Having potentially large market volumes may not be profitable either. Distribution may be inefficient or premium pricing inappropriate.

Therefore, take the time to consider all market forces and their effect on the true value of a market—before you file.

Global vs Local Idiosyncrasies

Are there any barriers to entry?

There may be some Freedom to Operate (FTO) issues with registered IP rights such as patents and trade mark registrations in some countries and not in others. Some countries may even prohibit the importation of your goods.

This information can be found from FTO searching, as will be discussed a lot more in Section 2 – Competitive Intelligence.

On the other hand, **some countries require you to have IP rights** before you can operate there.

IP laws vary around the world. **What is protectable in one country may not be protectable in another**. For example, as discussed under "Patentable Subject Matter", China and Europe are not as lenient in relation to patenting software as the United States and Australia. Further, many Asian countries do not recognise brand rights gained through use and reputation and rely only upon registered trade mark rights.

Assessing what levels of IP protection are achievable is best done by an IP specialist. However, to provide you with some patent subject matter guidelines, I have included a table in the Technology Section.

Have there been any recent changes in IP law?

IP rights change constantly, albeit slowly. What may have once been patentable or registrable may not be now, and vice versa. Fees, timings, grace periods, routes to protection, and penalties are constantly in a state of flux.

For example, there are "group" rights available such as international patent applications (PCT), international trade mark applications (Madrid protocol), international design applications (Hague convention), and the European unitary patent. Many members leave and join these groups, which can lead to "grandfathering" procedures and possibly convoluted paths to protection.

Make sure to discuss filing strategies with a professional who is fully up to date with current IP law.

Pulling it all together

Considering the above, the next thing to do is prepare a list of countries, ranking them by priority. Refine your ranking after consulting with an IP specialist in collaboration with your marketing team.

From there, get ballpark figures for filing and ongoing costs in each country. Your IP budget will help determine how far down the priority list you can go before it becomes financially unfeasible to file. It can be tough to accept, but you may have to leave certain countries off your filing list.

Of course, if your first steps towards galactic domination come to fruition, the next innovation may be more far-reaching.

THE FOUR QUARTERS OF COMPETITIVE EDGE

"Opportunities come infrequently. When it rains gold, put out the bucket, not the thimble.."

WARREN BUFFET, AMERICAN BUSINESSMAN, INVESTOR, AND PHILANTHROPIST

From an IP perspective, competitive advantages can be grouped into Four Quarters with each quarter protected by different formal or informal mechanisms, making it easier to identify and safeguard your Competitive Edge.

Brand – the most valuable IP; often encapsulated in trade mark registrations and supported by good systems.

Operations and information – the backbone of any business; tricky to protect formally, relying upon relationships and good internal practices.

Technological advances – cool inventions which are covered by patents and trade secrets and which are sometimes open-sourced.

Design – aesthetic creations whether in stylistic shape or patterns and afforded protection through copyright or design registrations.

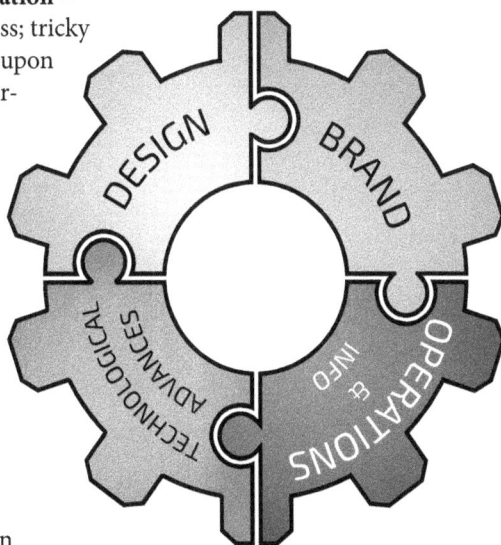

Protecting and maximising the value of a product or process often requires a multi-faceted approach that leverages the complementary strengths of various intellectual property laws and systems.

This is why I am passionate about my specialist field of IP strategy. It takes a comprehensive, helicopter view of an organisation. Intellectual property rights cannot be considered in isolation. An effective IP strategy identifies multiple issues, recognises the connections between them, and coordinates the relevant experts across various IP fields to deliver the specialised support required. This approach minimises overlap and provides greater context for the experts, as well as helping businesses to better understand and value the advice they receive.

The synergies created by integrating different protection and exploitation mechanisms across a range of competitive advantages can be remarkable. This is one of the reasons I wrote a book that goes across all intangible assets.

The story of Coca-Cola® showcases how the four Quarters can work synergistically to create great value.

The multi-pronged IP story of Coca-Cola

Coca-Cola's success story illustrates how strategic use of intellectual property can transform a product that might have remained a low-cost commodity into a global business powerhouse with a market capitalization of $310 billion as of 2024.

Coca-Cola was developed in the 1880s as a temperance drink and nerve tonic. Its original formula contained cocaine from the coca leaf and caffeine from the kola nut, which inspired its name. Although the combination of these ingredients could have been patented for the synergistic effects at the time, Coca-Cola chose instead to protect its formula as a trade secret—an IP strategy that lasts as long as the secret remains undisclosed. (Internal Systems to protect Technology)

When Coca-Cola first emerged, there were many similar tonics with similar names on the market. It took significant investment in both time and money for the company to consolidate its position and overcome these competitors. This highlights why in the next section I emphasise the value of choosing a distinctive mark from the start.

In the early days, carbonated drinks were made on-site in drugstores by mixing syrup with soda fountain water, which limited where and when consumers could enjoy the beverage. Coca-Cola revolutionized the industry in the 1890s by inventing and patenting a bottling process, allowing the company to distribute their drinks far beyond the soda fountains, first across the United States and eventually around the world. (Patents protecting Technology)

The company's iconic bottle design also played a crucial role. Registered in the 1920s, the bottle went through several iterations before becoming so distinctive that it gained trade mark protection in the 1970s. (Design being protected through Trade Mark law)

Beyond patents and trade marks, Coca-Cola has built a broad portfolio of IP rights, including copyright for its

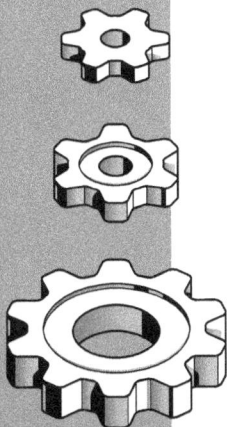

advertising jingles, digital content, and ownership of key domain names to protect its online presence and prevent poaching of similar website names (aka cybersquatting). (Brand and copyright)

Without these strategic IP protections, Coca-Cola might have remained just another beverage supplier. Instead, by securing and leveraging these rights, the company has been able to maintain its competitive edge and grow into the global giant it is today.

Coca-Cola exemplifies how clever use of multiple IP rights can grow a business—even if it is based on a commodity.

Now we look at perhaps the most well-known of all intangible assets: brand.

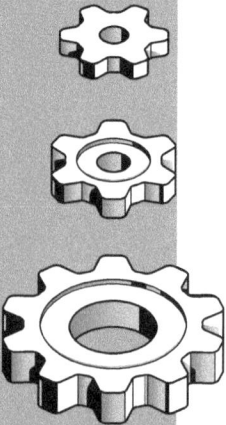

QUARTER 1
BRAND

"Your brand is what people say about you
when you're not in the room."

JEFF BEZOS - AMAZON FOUNDER

Brand is perhaps the most accessible of all intangible assets—something we instinctively understand. We each carry a personal brand or style, and our preferences for certain products or services are often not driven by superiority, but by emotional resonance. They feel right to us.

In today's hyper-connected world, relentless digital messaging and consumer culture have made brand omnipresent. We're logo-literate and brand-conscious—sporting designer clothing, driving badge-laden vehicles, and showcasing personal tech that speaks volumes about who we are or aspire to be.

Yet despite its ubiquity, brand as an asset remains underutilised. Many organisations still underestimate how to build, protect, and fully leverage brand value.

This quarter of the Competitive Edge cog explores:

✓ How brand value and goodwill are realised

✓ What elements make up a brand and how these can be protected

✓ How to select a distinctive and registrable trade mark

✓ The trade mark registration process

✓ The consequences of trade mark infringement

✓ And a touch of fun—how to avoid crossing the line into having an offensive trade mark.

Known global brand stories are used to illustrate each point, but it's important to note: brand does not exist in isolation. It relies heavily on the integrity of your operations—the systems, processes, and people that consistently deliver on the brand promise. These interdependencies are what power a truly sustainable competitive edge.

The above is why I recommend that if brand provides your competitive edge, you also read about Operations in this book.

3

LOVING BRANDS

"Creating Lovemarks is all about the ability to understand consumers' dreams, to know what they want and when they want it, and to create great experiences that make your brand a part of their lives."

KEVIN ROBERTS, FORMER GLOBAL CEO OF SAATCHI & SAATCHI, AND LOVEMARKS® AUTHOR

The tech geek in me loves shiny new things (aka inventions), so it is galling to admit that eventually the most valuable intangible asset of a business will be brand.

Early in my career, an appreciation of brand was cultured in me by having Kevin Roberts, the former global CEO of Saatchi & Saatchi, as a mentor. Over dinner, he once sketched out his Lovemarks philosophy for me on a napkin, and I even had the honour of being quoted in his Lovemarks book.

In essence, a business or a person becomes a "Lovemark" if they inspire "Loyalty Beyond Reason"—a powerful concept I've aimed to achieve throughout my career. It is also a tangibly valuable concept which, in 2006, won Saatchi & Saatchi a $US430 million JC Penney contract.

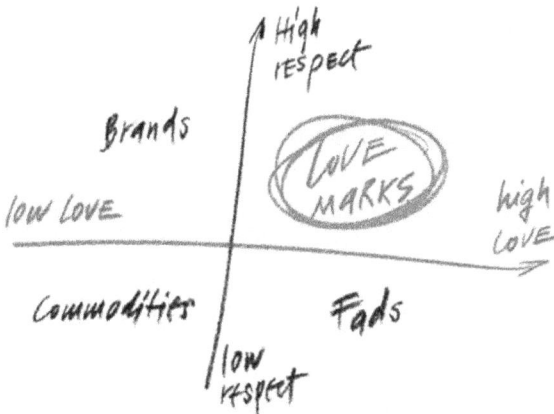

Brand value is something that can be measured—and there are various methods to do so. Interbrand®, for instance, is a well-known company that assesses the value of the world's top brands. Their valuation method focuses on three key areas:

✓ Financial performance of the branded products or services

✓ The role the brand plays in purchase decisions

✓ The brand's competitive strength and its ability to foster loyalty, which drives sustainable demand and profit over time.

If you look at Interbrand's 2024 rankings below, brand value is no small matter. Consider that just the Apple brand (not including the products) is valued at just under half a trillion US dollars!

01	02	03	04	05
(Apple)	Microsoft	amazon	Google	SAMSUNG
-3%	+11%	+8%	+12%	+10%
488.9 $B	352.5 $B	298.1 $B	291.3 $B	100.8 $B

06	07	08	09	10
Toyota	Coca-Cola	Mercedes	McDonald's	BMW
+13%	+5%	-4%	+4%	+2%
72.8 $B	61.2 $B	58.9 $B	53.0 $B	52.0 $B

11	12	13	14	15
LOUIS VUITTON	TESLA	CISCO	Nike	Instagram
+9%	-9%	+5%	-5%	+15%
50.9 $B	45.5 $B	45.5 $B	45.4 $B	45.1 $B

16	17	18	19	20
Disney	Adobe	ORACLE	IBM	SAP
-1%	+12%	+9%	+7%	+11%
42.8 $B	39.4 $B	37.7 $B	37.3 $B	36.8 $B

21	22	23	24	25
(Facebook)	HERMÈS	CHANEL	YouTube	J.P.Morgan
+10%	+15%	+7%	+16%	+5%
34.9 $B	34.7 $B	33.2 $B	30.1 $B	27.1 $B

This chart compares the movement of each 2024 brand value with where it was in 2023 by showing +/- percentage values.

As you can see from the shifts in percentage, actual brand value can vary significantly in just one year. Some tips for sustaining brand value follow.

4

SUSTAINING BRAND VALUE

"It takes many good deeds to build a good reputation, and only one bad one to lose it."
BENJAMIN FRANKLIN, FOUNDING FATHER OF THE UNITED STATES

Brand value is fragile; it can be easily damaged. A single negative news story can drastically change consumer perceptions. Every day, our choices are influenced by the brands we trust, from the groceries we buy to the cars we drive. Often, our choice is based not on price alone, but a brand's reputation and our experience of that brand.

Building brand value is a long-term commitment. When I create IP strategies, I am always thinking about ways to create barriers for competitors. This gives the business time to gain a foothold in a new market and establish its brand. A phrase I use to explain this to clients is providing "Cause to Pause".

To build a strong brand, businesses must first understand what their brand represents.

✓ What values does it embody?

✓ What is its personality?

✓ Is it playful, serious, dependable, luxurious, or rugged?

✓ How does the brand present itself to employees and the public?

✓ Is this identity consistent?

A business must also have robust internal systems to deliver on its brand promise. Consistency is key—both internally and externally. A brand might evolve over time, but it must remain authentic and true to the essence of the business.

A brand guide can help here. Typically, this is a document that encompasses aspects such as culture, wording, fonts, colours, logos, and the placement of brand elements on marketing materials, including product packaging.

Building brand value takes time, but the payoff can be immense when a brand resonates with its audience. Likewise, the payoff can be immense when a business is sold, and the brand value translates to the goodwill portion of the business sale.

Therefore, be mindful of the actions that your business takes and look for opportunities to enhance your brand at every opportunity.

5

GOODWILL

"As I often remind our analysts, 100% of the information you have about a company represents the past, and 100% of the value depends on the future."
– BILL MILLER, AMERICAN INVESTOR

Goodwill is essentially the reputation, customer loyalty, brand recognition, and trust that a business builds over time. It is what keeps customers coming back, even when competitors offer something cheaper or flashier. It's also what allows a business to charge a premium and still retain market share.

In accounting terms, goodwill usually appears on the balance sheet only after a business is sold. That is because it is often calculated as the difference between the sale price and the total value of the tangible (and some intangible) assets.

In older businesses, goodwill is usually the largest component of the sale price. A buyer isn't just purchasing stock and fittings—they're investing in the ongoing relationships, the reputation, and the assurance that the brand will continue to deliver.

Goodwill doesn't exist in isolation. It's often built upon—and protected by—a combination of intellectual property rights: trade marks, design registrations, even copyright in brand elements like jingles or packaging. These work together to maintain the brand's image and protect it from imitation, helping to preserve that elusive but essential business asset.

A trusted brand can even outlast temporary financial troubles if the goodwill remains strong, as can be illustrated by the case of Sara Lee*.

A Sweet Tale

When McCain Foods acquired the iconic frozen dessert brand Sara Lee Australia in 2013, the deal wasn't primarily about manufacturing facilities or inventory. It was about the strong brand equity Sara Lee had built in the Australian and New Zealand markets over decades.

Known for its cheesecakes and desserts, Sara Lee was a household name. The goodwill—customer loyalty, brand recognition, and positive associations—was a major component of the purchase price. Even when the brand entered voluntary administration in 2023, it remained attractive to buyers largely because of that enduring goodwill and as a consequence was bought in 2024 by a private company owned by Klark and Brooke Quinn.

The Quinns were also involved in the purchase of Australian confectionery maker Darrell Lea out of voluntary administration in 2012.

Due to the Quinns' action and the longevity of strong brands despite short-term financial issues, the Sara Lee and Darrell Lea brands can still be found in supermarkets today.

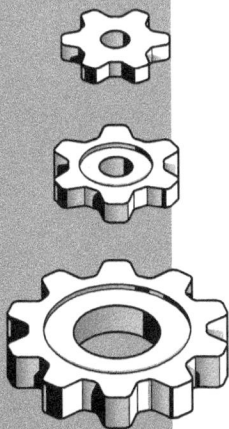

6

TYPES OF TRADE MARKS

"Your smile is your logo, your personality is your business card, how you leave others feeling after having an experience with you becomes your trade mark."

JAY DANZIE, AUTHOR, BRAND STRATEGIST, AND SPEAKER

A trade mark is how a business expresses its brand to consumers. While word marks are the most common form, many other elements can be registered as trade marks, including slogans, logos, shapes, sounds, smells, and even colours—as long as they meet the necessary criteria.

Single Words

The best single-word trade marks are distinctive and do not directly describe the product or service they represent. A great example is Sunsilk® shampoo. The name evokes the smooth, silky feel of the product without explicitly saying that it is shampoo.

"Apple" is another brilliant example of a common word used for a completely unrelated product. While "Apple" would be a poor trade mark for fruit, it's globally recognised when applied to innovative products like the iPhone®, iPad®, and Mac® computers. The Apple® trade mark is synonymous with cutting-edge technology and sleek design, commanding immense loyalty in the tech industry.

Similarly, Amazon® started as an online bookstore but chose its name from the Amazon River to reflect the company's expansive vision.

When "Brandstorming"® with clients, one of my preferred starting points is looking at mythological names which can also lend depth to a brand.

Nike®, for example, is derived from the Greek goddess of victory—perfect for a brand that embodies sports performance. Nike also has several other brand elements (discussed later), all of which are registered as trade marks and vigorously protected, contributing to its 2024 brand valuation of US$53 billion.

Nonsense words, like Kodak®, are another powerful trade mark option. A more modern example is Google®, which originated from a misspelling of "googol", meaning 10 to the power of 100. Google has become so entrenched in our culture that it's now a verb, symbolizing the brand's vast influence on the internet and technology sectors.

Slogans

Slogans can convey a brand's personality even more effectively than a single word. However, registering a slogan as a trade mark can be tricky since many are common phrases that trade mark law aims to keep free for public use.

For example, the phrases "Have a Nice Day" and "Made with Love" should be available for all to use.

To be eligible for trade mark protection, a slogan must be distinctive and closely associated with specific goods or services. Crafting a slogan that reflects a brand's core values and resonates with the market often requires significant marketing investment to gain the necessary recognition.

For newer businesses, a cost-effective approach is to register a strong, distinctive word mark and build recognition for the slogan through marketing efforts. Over time, if the slogan gains enough reputation, it can also be registered as a trade mark.

For example, the following slogans are innocuous phrases but arising from a consistent and heavy investment in marketing, they have become synonymous with the organisations that promote them.

"Just Do It" – Nike

"I'm Lovin' It" – McDonald's

"Because You're Worth It" – L'Oréal

"Finger Lickin' Good" – KFC

"A Diamond is Forever" – De Beers

"We Try Harder" – Avis

"The Happiest Place on Earth" – Disneyland

Logos

If you glance at Interbrand's brand valuation table, I'm confident you can identify most companies just by their logos. A great logo stands alone, with no need for the company's name beside it. It serves a purpose where a word mark might be less impactful—like on a car badge or grille.

Many logos also have stories behind them, adding to their brand personality. For instance, Tesla®'s stylized "T" represents the cross-section of an electric motor, highlighting its focus on electric vehicles.

Toyota®'s logo of overlapping ellipses symbolizes the connection between the company and its customers.

The Nike "Swoosh" is a simple yet powerful logo that conveys motion and success—fitting for a brand that dominates the athletic world. It is also said to have been derived from the curvature of a feather on the goddess Nike's wing.

Even an evolving logo can have longevity.

| 1976 | 1977 | 1998 | 1999 | 2007 | NOW |

Three-Dimensional Marks

Sometimes, a product's shape is so distinctive that it serves as a brand mark in its own right. When this happens, the three-dimensional shape can be registered as a trade mark. As discussed earlier, the iconic Coca-Cola bottle is one of the most famous examples of a 3D trade mark. Another notable example is the Rolls-Royce® grille.

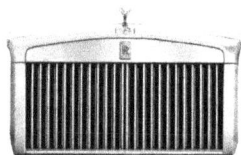

Even more humble products can have unique shapes that are protected by 3D trade marks, underscoring the importance of distinctiveness in brand identity.

Meet the humble kiwifruit vine tie

Kiwifruit is one of New Zealand's larger exports, generating around US$1.8 billion annually. The vines are secured to overhead trellises using vine ties, like the ones shown below. This particular design is highly effective, with the end hooks easily locking over the trellis wires. The manufacturer, Klipon®, produced this design under the trade mark Kiwiklip®, and enjoyed a 16-year monopoly on the shape of the vine tie due to a quirk in New Zealand copyright law.

However, once that 16-year term expired, the copyright protection ended, allowing any company to manufacture and sell identical vine ties. This was potentially disastrous as the market was significant—as evidenced by Klipon having already produced over a billion vine ties by this point!

Concerned about increased competition, Klipon sought advice from my previous firm to explore their options. The creative solution (at the time) was to file for a 3D trade mark to protect the actual shape of the vine tie. Given their established reputation and the strong association consumers had with the product, we were able to demonstrate that the shape of the vine tie was distinctly linked to Klipon. With over a billion ties in circulation, this reputation certainly worked in the manufacturers' favour.

The 3D trade mark registration ensured that Klipon could maintain a perpetual monopoly on their design, as long as they continued paying the renewal fees every 10 years. This strategy allowed them to secure their market position long after the original copyright protection expired.

Colour

A colour mark can be powerful as a brand as it can be applied to many parts of a product or its packaging, recognised at a distance and quickly, without the consumer having to take time to read the company name.

Certain colour hues or combinations can also be registered as trade marks, but when applying for registration, the applicant must take care to specify exactly which shades are being claimed and how they apply to the product or marketing materials.

The trade mark applicant must also be able to show that it has significant reputation in its colour scheme.

Securing a trade mark for a colour can be challenging, and disputes over colour rights are not uncommon. For instance, Cadbury®, Nestlé®, and Whittaker's® have long battled over the exclusive use of the colour purple in their chocolate packaging.

A great example of a colour trade mark is John Deere's iconic green and yellow colour combination on its tractors. This colour scheme is recognised worldwide and is protected by trade mark registrations in numerous countries.

Sound

The roar of a lion at the beginning of films produced by Metro-Goldwyn-Mayer is one of the most iconic sounds in cinema history.

Sound is not typically the first thing that comes to mind when we think about trade marks, but certain sounds are instantly recognisable and closely associated with specific brands. Here are some famous examples:

Nokia tune: Derived from Francisco Tárrega's composition "Grande Valse", this melody became the default ringtone for Nokia phones and is globally recognised.

Intel Bong: The five-note jingle from Intel is one of the most recognisable sound trade marks, indicating the presence of Intel processors in computers.

McDonald's "I'm Lovin' It": This five-note jingle is part of a larger marketing campaign, but it has become synonymous with the McDonald's brand worldwide.

Netflix Tudum: The distinctive sound that plays when starting a show or film on Netflix is instantly recognisable and has become an auditory hallmark of the streaming service.

Harley-Davidson engine rev: The Harley-Davidson motorcycle engine's distinctive sound was once the subject of a trade mark application.

20th Century Fox Fanfare: The grand, dramatic fanfare that plays before 20th Century Fox films is one of the most recognisable sound cues in the film industry.

Greensleeves arrangement: A particular arrangement of this tune (apocryphally attributed to King Henry VIII) as used by Mr Whippy to lure children to buy soft-serve ice cream is registered as a trade mark.

Scent

Unexpectedly, scent can be a registrable trade mark.

Close your eyes, think of Play-Doh®, breathe deep and remember that scent from childhood. This scent has been registered since the 1990s and is described as a "unique fragrance formed through a combination of a sweet, slightly musky, vanilla-like fragrance, with slight overtones of cherry, and the natural smell of a salted, wheat-based dough."

As Play-Doh had been around in abundance since 1955, the dough scent had acquired enough reputation to be registered.

Another fascinating example, although now lapsed, was a New Zealand trade mark application for gin with the following description:

"The trade mark is a scent comprising the smell of the rainforest of the West Coast of the South Island of New Zealand, specifically consisting of a Head Note of citrus (lemon peel) and Tarata and Douglas fir, which continues approximately two seconds from exposure to the scent; a Heart Note of sweet, deep pine resin from Douglas fir, Rimu and Totara, which continues for about one second after the disappearance of the Head Note; and a sweet, spiced Base Note of cardamom and cassia, which continues for about three seconds."

Trade Dress

Trade dress refers to the visual appearance or design elements of a business or product that help consumers recognise its brand without seeing a name or logo. Imagine walking into an unfamiliar store, yet being able to identify it just by its layout, colour scheme, and design. That's trade dress.

Trade dress is commonly used in the retail and hospitality industries and can cover everything from the store layout to furniture design, colour schemes, and even the style of counters and menus. In many countries, trade dress can be registered under trade mark laws, provided it is distinctive enough and meets the necessary criteria for registration.

A single organisation, product or service can have a multiplicity of brand elements by which they are recognised. Identifying, protecting and using these elements well can build significant brand value within an organisation.

A brand experience

One of my more memorable IP excursions was to visit the headquarters of John Deere® (a client of mine at the time).

They are located (naturally) at 1 John Deere drive in Moline, a small city in Illinois, about an hour's flight from Chicago.

The brand impact of John Deere in this community is massive. The town has John Deere Pavilion, John Deere Historic Site, John Deere Tractor & Engine Museum, and John Deere World Headquarters.

Most of the merchandising in the tiny Moline airport is John Deere related. I even bought a book there called 101 Uses for an Old John Deere, by Cletus Hohman!

When I turned up for my meeting, I taxied through extensive, immaculately manicured grounds, which were densely populated with green and yellow ground-care machinery.

Everything in the headquarters also screamed the JD brand.

I loved how they lived their iconic brand in everything they did. A lesson for many of us.

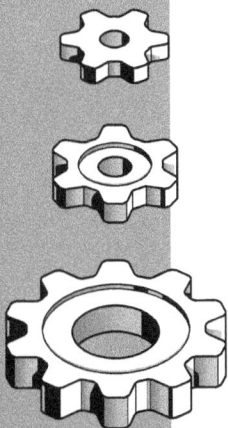

7

CHOOSING A TRADE MARK

"Brand is just a perception, and
perception will match reality over time."
ELON MUSK, CEO OF TESLA AND SPACEX

While I recommend that a brand strategist is consulted to develop your brand, an appreciation of the associated IP issues is essential to avoid costly mistakes.

The best trade marks, both from a marketing and registrability perspective, are distinctive and non-descriptive. Fuller criteria for registrable trade marks are discussed in Chapter 8.

A good trade mark should stand out from competitors and avoid causing confusion in the market. The trade mark rights must also be robust enough to deter competitors from adopting a similar mark, or to be enforceable if infringement occurs.

Establishing a valuable global brand can become an uphill battle, requiring significant time, money, and effort. Most businesses, especially those in the early stages or launching a new project, do not have the resources or resilience to endure such challenges.

Be smart and do your research (discussed in the Competitive Intelligence section) before committing to one of the most critical business decisions you'll make—choosing what will likely become your most valuable asset: your brand.

Start with Basic Research

Search online for your preferred trade marks, and investigate any existing rights in your intended markets. If you're working with a brand strategist, challenge them to come up with a trade mark that is distinctive and protectable while also reflecting the personality of the business.

You may settle on a single trade mark or preferably have several trade marks that you like. If you rank those marks in order of your personal preference, then an IP professional (preferably a registered trade mark attorney) can work their way down the list, stopping when they find the highest-ranked mark which is available for use and registration. They can also advise whether your chosen mark is viable in your preferred markets, considering local laws and other trade mark owners.

My preferred approach is to do what I call Brandstorming®. This is working in real time with clients as we debate the merits of the various trade marks we dream up, and checking out potential infringement and registrability issues through trade mark searching. The criteria for registrability are discussed in the next chapter.

I strongly advocate for getting professional advice because I've seen many examples of businesses investing heavily in a new brand—producing extensive marketing materials, hosting a big launch—only to be hit with a cease-and-desist order shortly thereafter.

8

CRITERIA FOR TRADE MARK REGISTRATION

"Learn the rules like a pro, so you can break them like an artist."

PABLO PICASSO, SPANISH ARTIST AND FATHER OF CUBISM

For a trade mark to be registered, it must meet specific criteria. These criteria ensure that a trade mark can serve its primary purpose—distinguishing the goods or services of one business from another—while also preventing the granting of excessive rights to trade mark applicants.

When filing a trade mark application, one or more of 45 goods and/or service classes are nominated. Essentially, class nomination indicates how you are using or intend to use your trade mark. This system allows owners of the same trade mark to co-exist in unrelated businesses, effectively opening up the availability of marks for use and registration.

For example, the ACORN® mark has been registered separately for stair lifts (class 7) and investment services (class 36) by different parties. This is allowed as there is no overlap of the activities by the different parties.

Here are some of the key requirements:

Distinctiveness

A trade mark must be capable of identifying the products or services as coming from a particular source, setting them apart from those of others. Distinctiveness can be either inherent (naturally unique) or acquired (becoming distinctive through extensive use). Acquired distinctiveness is a more expensive route to take, so choose an inherently distinctive mark!

Non-Descriptive

A trade mark must not describe the goods or services it represents. It should not directly refer to the quality, intended purpose, value, geographical origin, or other characteristics. For example, "Super Clean" for a cleaning service would likely be too descriptive to be registrable unless it gained distinctiveness through use.

Not Deceptive or Misleading

A trade mark must not deceive or mislead consumers about the nature, quality, or origin of the goods or services. For instance, a mark implying a product is made in Italy when it is not is likely to be unregistrable.

Freedom to Operate

The trade mark should not conflict with any prior rights. It must not be identical or confusingly similar to existing trade marks registered in related classes of goods or services. Trade mark offices will conduct searches to ensure new marks do not infringe existing rights. Also consider non-registered rights based on reputation as part of your Competitive Intelligence research.

No Public Policy or Morality Issues

The trade mark should not conflict with public policy or accepted principles of morality. Offensive or derogatory terms or images would generally be refused. This is a highly subjective judgement and some of the principles are discussed on the following page.

OFFENSIVE TRADE MARKS

Many New Zealanders will remember the iconic Toyota HiLux "Bugger" ads, which first aired on national TV in 1999, starring Hercules the dog along with his unfortunate farmer owner. Although most viewers found these advertisements humorous and reflective of Kiwi culture, they were briefly pulled following 120 public complaints. However, the advertisements were later reinstated after the Broadcasting Standards Authority deemed them not offensive.

When the same advertisement ran in Australia, with its five times larger population, there was only one complaint! (I suspect it was from a visiting New Zealander.) This highlights an interesting cultural difference between the two nations but also illustrates that acceptability of a brand is market specific.

Trade Marks Acts in most countries allow for the refusal of "offensive" marks. In New Zealand, this includes marks that are considered offensive to Māori, as judged by a specialised committee.

So, what is considered acceptable? In New Zealand, several marks incorporating the word "Bugger" have been registered for various goods and services, including:

BUGGA OFF

FUSSY BUGGAS

TASTY BUGGERS

LAZY BUGGER

SAUCY BUGGER

BUGGER CAFÉ

Clearly, the New Zealand Intellectual Property Office (IPONZ) does not find the term "Bugger" offensive enough to refuse registration.

So, when considering whether to use a potentially offensive word or phrase in marketing, it's important to think about:

Purpose – Is the word meant to enhance the brand's culture, engage the audience, or simply raise a smile? Or is it being used gratuitously?

Audience – Is the term acceptable to your target audience, and does it serve its intended purpose?

Registrability – Do you want exclusive use of the term? If so, be aware of trade mark registration guidelines and whether the mark could be refused for being offensive.

10

THE TRADE MARK
REGISTRATION PROCESS

Obtaining formal IP rights follows a similar process in most parts of the world. Below is an overview of the key stages in the trade mark registration process:

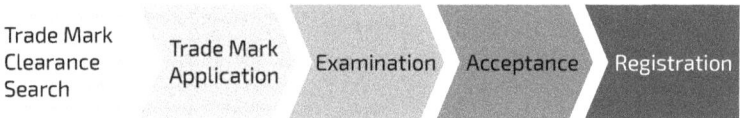

Trade Mark Clearance Search → Trade Mark Application → Examination → Acceptance → Registration

Trade Mark Searching

Discussed in greater detail in the next section, conducting initial competitive intelligence on its chosen brand is important for a business. This helps rule out poor options early on. However, before fully committing to a trade mark and investing in marketing collateral, I highly recommend having a final, professional search conducted by an IP specialist. This ensures that the mark is not only distinctive but also free from conflicts with existing trade marks.

Penalties for trade mark infringement are discussed later in Chapter 12.

Trade Mark Application

Trade mark applications can be filed with the relevant trade mark office by anyone. However, I strongly advise using an IP specialist to avoid costly mistakes.

Two questions to consider when filing:

1. **What mark are you applying for?**

   It is a rookie mistake to include too many elements in a trade mark application, which can reduce the scope of protection. Infringement is often judged based on the mark as a whole rather than individual elements—unless a particular element is highly distinctive.

For example:

- ✓ A single distinctive word mark should be filed in plain text to cover all fonts.
- ✓ A distinctive logo should be filed separately from the word mark. For instance, the John Deere logo stands alone without words.
- ✓ Ordinary, unregistrable words should be excluded. For example, file for KODAK rather than KODAK film.

2. What classes of goods and services are you filing in?

Trade mark registration only grants rights in relation to the specific goods and services listed in the application. You cannot register across all classes unless you genuinely use or intend to use the mark in those areas. Importantly, a trade mark can be struck off for non-use.

These classes fall into the following categories:

CLASS	CATEGORY	GENERAL DESCRIPTION
1	Goods	Chemicals used in industry, science and photography, as well as in agriculture
2	Goods	Paints, varnishes, lacquers; preservatives against rust and deterioration of wood
3	Goods	Cleaning, polishing, scouring and abrasive preparations
4	Goods	Industrial oils and greases; lubricants; dust absorbing, wetting and binding compositions
5	Goods	Pharmaceutical and veterinary preparations; sanitary preparations for medical use
6	Goods	Common metals and their alloys; metal building materials
7	Goods	Machines and machine tools; motors and engines (except for land vehicles)
8	Goods	Hand tools and implements (hand-operated); cutlery; razors
9	Goods	Scientific, nautical, surveying, photographic, cinematographic, optical, weighing, measuring, signalling, checking apparatus and instruments
10	Goods	Medical apparatus and instruments

CLASS	CATEGORY	GENERAL DESCRIPTION
11	Goods	Apparatus for lighting, heating, steam generating, cooking, refrigerating, drying, ventilating, water supply and sanitary purposes
12	Goods	Vehicles; apparatus for locomotion by land, air or water
13	Goods	Firearms; ammunition and projectiles; explosives; fireworks
14	Goods	Precious metals and their alloys; jewellery, precious stones; horological and chronometric instruments
15	Goods	Musical instruments
16	Goods	Paper, cardboard and goods made from these materials; printed matter; bookbinding material
17	Goods	Rubber, gutta-percha, gum, asbestos, mica and goods made from these materials
18	Goods	Leather and imitations of leather; animal skins and hides; trunks and travelling bags
19	Goods	Building materials (non-metallic); non-metallic rigid pipes for building; asphalt, pitch and bitumen
20	Goods	Furniture, mirrors, picture frames; goods not included in other classes made of wood, cork, reed, cane
21	Goods	Household or kitchen utensils and containers; combs and sponges
22	Goods	Ropes, string, nets, tents, awnings, tarpaulins, sails, sacks and bags
23	Goods	Yarns and threads, for textile use
24	Goods	Textiles and textile goods, not included in other classes; bed and table covers
25	Goods	Clothing, footwear, headgear
26	Goods	Lace and embroidery, ribbons and braid; buttons, hooks and eyes, pins and needles
27	Goods	Carpets, rugs, mats and matting, linoleum and other materials for covering existing floors

CLASS	CATEGORY	GENERAL DESCRIPTION
28	Goods	Games and playthings; gymnastic and sporting articles not included in other classes
29	Goods	Meat, fish, poultry and game; meat extracts
30	Goods	Coffee, tea, cocoa, sugar, rice, tapioca, sago, artificial coffee
31	Goods	Agricultural, horticultural and forestry products; live animals; fresh fruits and vegetables
32	Goods	Beers; mineral and aerated waters and other non-alcoholic drinks
33	Goods	Alcoholic beverages (except beers)
34	Goods	Tobacco; smokers, articles; matches
35	Services	Advertising; business management; business administration; office functions
36	Services	Insurance; financial affairs; monetary affairs; real estate affairs
37	Services	Building construction; repair; installation services
38	Services	Telecommunications
39	Services	Transport; packaging and storage of goods; travel arrangement
40	Services	Treatment of materials
41	Services	Education; providing of training; entertainment; sporting and cultural activities
42	Services	Scientific and technological services and research and design
43	Services	Legal services; security services for the protection of property and individuals
44	Services	Services for providing food and drink; temporary accommodation
45	Services	Medical services; veterinary services; hygienic and beauty care

Think carefully about where your business is now and where you want it to go in the future. Apply in the appropriate classes accordingly.

Examination

Trade mark applications are examined by trained examiners in IP offices in each country they are filed. During examination, a trade mark examiner will:

✓ Check whether there are any existing marks on the register that might conflict with the application.

✓ Ensure that the mark is distinctive, non-descriptive, and non-offensive.

Acceptance/Registration

Once the examiner confirms that the trade mark meets all criteria, the application is accepted and advertised. This triggers an opposition period, typically lasting three months (and extendable), during which third parties can object to the registration.

If no successful opposition is raised, the trade mark is registered. This grants the owner the right to stop others from using confusingly similar marks in relation to the same goods and services within the country. The owner can even notify Customs authorities of these rights, who can then prevent imports bearing the registered rights from entering the country.

One of the best features of trade mark registration is that, unlike patents, trade marks can last forever—as long as renewal fees are paid on average every 10 years.

International Applications

Many countries are part of an International Convention, which allows you to file international trade mark applications within six months of the original filing date and backdate them to the original application.

Further, international applications can be filed either in individual countries or through an international agreement known as the Madrid Protocol, which enables a single application to cover multiple countries.

Unlike patents and design applications trade mark applications can be filed after a brand has been publicly disclosed, providing more flexibility in timing your protection efforts.

11

TRADE MARK INFRINGEMENT PENALTIES

"Lawsuit: A machine which you go into as a pig and come out of as a sausage."

AMBROSE BIERCE, AMERICAN JOURNALIST

Trade mark infringement is a serious matter. Businesses fiercely protect their trade mark rights, as infringement can damage their most valuable asset—their reputation. Courts treat these cases with similar gravity.

For example, in Adidas vs. Payless Shoesource (2008), Adidas was awarded $305 million in a trade mark infringement lawsuit, claiming that Payless was selling shoes with a design similar to its three-stripe mark. The award was later reduced to $65 million upon settlement, but this is still a significant sum.

Trade mark infringement and penalties vary depending on the country and case. However, common penalties include:

Monetary Damages:
The infringer may be required to pay for profits made from unauthorised use and compensate the trade mark owner for losses suffered. In some cases, additional damages may be awarded for wilful infringement.

Injunctions:
Courts can issue orders preventing further infringement, such as stopping the sale, production, or import of infringing goods.

Destruction of infringing goods:
Infringing items, including materials used to produce them, may be ordered to be destroyed or handed over.

Legal costs:

The infringer could be ordered to cover the trade mark owner's legal expenses.

Criminal penalties:

In serious cases, particularly those involving wilful infringement on a large scale, criminal charges may be brought, leading to fines and even imprisonment.

Corrective advertising:

The infringer might be required to fund advertising to correct any confusion caused by the infringement.

Border measures:

In some countries, customs authorities can seize infringing goods at the border to prevent their import or export.

Assignment of phone numbers:

In the past, phone numbers listed in printed directories could be reassigned from the infringer to the trade mark owner.

Trade mark protection is vital, and businesses need to be aware of the risks and penalties associated with infringement.

Conducting proper research and legal advice upfront can prevent costly legal battles down the road.

QUARTER 2
OPERATIONS AND INFORMATION

"We are what we repeatedly do.
Excellence, then, is not an act, but a habit."

ARISTOTLE, GREEK PHILOSOPHER AND POLYMATH

The term "I-Stuff", coined by Suzanne Harrison, co-author of Edison in the Boardroom and Einstein in the Boardroom, refers to intangible assets that are difficult to define, capture, and capitalise. While the phrase hasn't gained the recognition it perhaps deserves in the IP world, it aptly describes the hardest-to-pin-down aspects of organisational knowledge. Harrison wanted a term that covered tacit knowledge, know-how, relationships, and other uncodified organisational knowledge, without invoking financial or accounting connotations. Her book Einstein in the Boardroom explores how to manage and value this "I-Stuff".

When considering this Quarter of competitive edge, I decided to look beyond the broad definition of I-Stuff to focus on specific areas such as copyright, systems, confidentiality, culture, and security—along with the intriguing concept of negative know-how.

Operations are perhaps the least glamorous category of intangible assets. While they are the engine room of any commercial organisation, they are frequently overlooked and poorly managed from an IP perspective.

Strong internal systems also bolster brand value, supporting the delivery of brand promises like responsiveness, quality, price, creativity, and reliability.

An organisation that deals primarily in commodities, without clever inventions, can still thrive with good operational systems. On the other hand, a business with great inventions but weak operations will likely need external help to fully commercialise its innovations.

A global giant which started in a commodity market but successfully worked its multiple IP categories—particularly its systems—is McDonald's.

Do you want fries with that?

McDonald's is the apex predator among franchises, offering commoditised food—hamburgers and other fast-food items that many can (and do) replicate in various forms. Since its modest beginnings in 1940, it has expanded to over 39,000 "restaurants" in more than a hundred countries worldwide. The brand's value alone is estimated at US$191 billion, significantly outweighing the estimated value of its tangible assets at US$56 billion.

Macca's influence is so profound that it has inspired its own economic measure—the "Big Mac Index". Introduced by The Economist in 1986, this informal index measures purchasing power parity (PPP) between countries by comparing the cost of a Big Mac® hamburger in different regions. By converting Big Mac hamburger prices into a single currency (typically the US dollar), the index provides insight into whether a currency is over- or undervalued relative to the dollar.

Over the years, McDonald's has leveraged a portfolio of registered intellectual property rights, such as patents, design rights, and trade mark registrations, to maintain and strengthen its global position. However, patents and design rights are time-limited, and trade mark registrations alone cannot prevent competitors from offering remarkably similar products and services.

It is important to recognise that McDonald's unregistered IP and the protective measures surrounding it give the company a distinct advantage over new entrants in the market. McDonald's safeguards certain recipes and processes as trade secrets. The precise ingredients and methods used to produce its iconic sauces are closely guarded and protected through confidentiality agreements with suppliers and employees.

McDonald's also holds copyright in its advertising materials, training manuals, and promotional content. This encompasses commercials, print advertisements, training videos, and digital and social media campaigns.

I have established my own non-franchised restaurants and previously worked with McDonald's as their patent attorney in New Zealand. This has led me to believe McD's greatest strength is in unregistered IP, particularly with their ordering systems, meal preparation, and training methods.

12

FRANCHISES

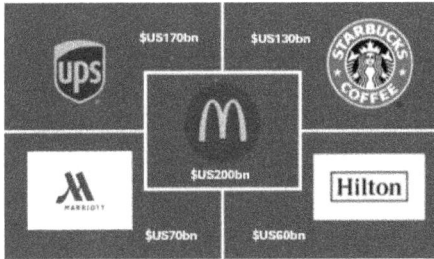

Estimated Market Caps 2024

Global franchises are prime examples of how good operational systems can scale a business model, even if the core product is something others can easily offer. Franchisees often pay for a bundle of intangible assets, including operational manuals and trade mark licences.

If a franchise's intangible assets are not protected by patents or trade mark registrations, they can be replicated by others without risking litigation. So why invest in a franchise, beyond brand recognition? The answer lies in gaining immediate access to proven operational systems.

Having set up various businesses virtually from scratch, I know firsthand that creating business systems is a substantial task. It requires careful planning, significant resources, skill, and ongoing effort to refine and maintain those systems.

For example, a small retail business might need a point-of-sale system, inventory management software, and basic accounting tools.

In contrast, a manufacturing company might integrate supply chain management, production scheduling, and customer relationship systems.

A professional services firm may require templated precedents, secure client data systems, and robust training protocols.

Developing, customising, and consistently implementing these systems takes time and involves risk. Purchasing a franchise offers instant access to these systems—along with immediate brand recognition, which can be worth the investment.

Franchise agreements are discussed in the Collaboration section.

Think carefully when you are considering becoming a franchisee as to what benefits you are paying for – exclusivity, trade secrets, brand recognition, business systems or... And then consider what it would take you (time, money and effort) to replicate those benefits.

13

RECOGNISING VALUABLE OPERATIONAL ASSETS

The sheer volume of data and systems within a business can feel overwhelming. Defining and assigning value to these assets from an operational rather than a financial perspective is even more challenging. Comprehending how to protect and capitalise upon these largely unregistrable assets can seem like an insurmountable task.

One way to tackle this is to flip the approach and start by considering the business's competitive edges from start to finish.

A manufacturing client of mine once rolled out several metres of a diagram showing their supply chain and operations. This visual map made it easy for me to examine each aspect—from on-farm practices and raw ingredient supply to ingredient drying, blending, packaging, marketing, and distribution. Some steps provided competitive advantages through in-house efficiencies, others through consumer preference, and some were simply industry-standard business-as-usual practices. None of the steps had registered IP protection.

This visual approach was invaluable, as it highlighted not only individual components but also how they interacted and shared common touch points. An IP strategy could then be built by identifying what was unique to them and how that related to revenue. As an established business with minimal R&D, their main focus was on securing operational advantages rather than exploring the forms of IP in the other three Competitive Edge Quarters.

14

PROTECTION MECHANISMS

Protecting I-Stuff involves thinking about how these intangible assets can be controlled and used. Various protection mechanisms are discussed in this section, but first it helps to approach the protection of intangible assets by imagining them as tangible, fragile objects that could be easily damaged or destroyed.

For example, if an organisation's value lies in producing and displaying rare and delicate vases, the protection steps could include:

✓ Educating the team about the value of the vases and how to handle them properly

✓ Limiting access to the most valuable vases, preventing general staff or customers from mishandling them

✓ Ensuring staff don't give vases away

✓ Having Standard Operating Procedures (SOPs) in place to ensure consistency in the manufacturing process, reducing the risk of breakages

✓ Caring for and retaining the vase designers

✓ Building an exclusive, high-end brand

✓ Taking action against counterfeit sellers

✓ Protecting the secret manufacturing process.

If you swap out the term "vases" with "intangible assets", then it becomes apparent that it is possible to protect the intangible, by visualising it appropriately.

This analogy underscores why IP awareness and fostering an IP-conscious culture are at the top of the list of protection mechanisms. Staff must understand, follow, and enforce the internal practices that preserve and enhance the value of intangible assets, especially those that cannot be safeguarded by formal legal means.

As IP concepts can be difficult to comprehend, choosing an analogy which relates directly to the actual operations of a business can communicate the concepts in a more relatable way.

15

IP AWARENESS
AND CULTURE

"Culture eats strategy for breakfast."

PETER DRUCKER, MANAGEMENT CONSULTANT, EDUCATOR, AND AUTHOR

Building IP awareness and foster-ing an IP-conscious culture within an organisation requires time, per-sistence, and an approach tailored to the company's unique needs.

Some organisations opt for struc-tured programs to enhance their inno-vation capabilities. Others take a more ad hoc route, bringing in experts to speak to staff or sending selected em-ployees on external courses.

Regardless of the method, it's important to acknowledge that staff turn-over and the evolving nature of the IP and innovation landscape are con-stants. Organisations that value their intangible assets must create an envi-ronment where these assets are easily recognised and appreciated and include ongoing team education.

It's equally important that key external players, such as suppliers, dis-tributors, and board members, also understand the value of these assets and act accordingly. For example, a supplier who works with multiple cus-tomers could unintentionally share competitive insights from one custom-er with another.

Intellectual property can easily be lost through careless handling. I've overheard sensitive and potentially valuable information being discussed in public places like airport lounges, planes, or restaurants. Notably, taxi drivers, many of whom have alternative careers in unexpected fields, often find themselves exposed to competitive intelligence unwittingly shared by passengers.

Fostering an awareness of the organisation's intangible asset value and ensuring appropriate behaviour within your organisation and with your external relationships is essential for safeguarding these assets.

Maxwell Smart's cone of silence would be a handy invention to have!

Within an innovative business, there is often a spectrum of personality types, each with something to contribute to the business. However, each has a differing mindset and often clashing views around innovation, commercialisation, and intellectual property. Only when there is an alignment among the participants within the business can there be a cultural shift towards embracing innovation that leads to a significant increase in organisational value.

Those engaged in helping the innovation community often identify two key and often disparate personality types they work with: scientists and engineers on the one hand, and entrepreneurs on the other.

Scientists and engineers often see intellectual property mainly as patents and scientists in particular value peer recognition and publication impact over commercialisation. Some feel IP conflicts with their values.in contrast, entrepreneurs less familiar with the R&D process view intellectual property as a broader business tool beyond just patents.

Strategic planning often occurs at a board level, and many methodologies have been developed to implement this. However, boards are often not well represented by scientists and entrepreneurs, who work more at an operational rather than governance level. Consequently, lofty ambitions expressed at board level for implementing an innovation culture may not be readily adopted by those at the coalface.

Therefore, to implement an innovative culture that is accepted, I recommend a vision is developed that all parties can agree upon.

The vision must:

✓ Define the scope within which the business operates
✓ Include at least one quality/value important to the business
✓ Align with key stakeholders
✓ Be measurable
✓ Be adaptable into an actionable strategic plan, including an IP strategic plan, if applicable.

Side Story

Culture beyond a Petri dish

One approach that inculcated IP culture within a national research organisation follows.

At one point, I managed a very large IP portfolio for a research organisation. The careers of many of the researchers started when research was purely for the "public good." In those days, research wasn't done primarily with commercial gain in mind, it was simply shared freely with the hope being that the outcomes of the research would be used by interested parties and hence create positive impact on a national level.

In 1992 the New Zealand government converted their research organisations to a much more "user pays" system where success was also measured by profit and deals done. However, such commercial drivers and the need for formal and active commercialisation was often seen by researchers as tainting the purity of scientific research. Management faced some resistance, and the idea of market directed research, especially for commercial gain and requiring restricted access was uncomfortable for many who valued academic freedom.

Despite this, the organisation was rich in both obvious and potential yet untapped intangible assets. My mission was to enable them to make the most of those assets—without ruffling feathers. We focused on understanding what motivated researchers and the environments in which they thrived. For most, motivation stemmed from the desire to continue their research and contribute to the public good. The environment in which the scientists operated i fostered a collegial atmosphere, which was important to consider.

With this in mind ,we used IP education to increase the awareness of IP, how to recognise and capture IP, and then showing how it could be leveraged to attract funding—ultimately allowing researchers to carry on with their work.

We embraced the collegial environment, hosting informal "brown bag" lunches for casual discussions about IP alongside structured but interactive workshops where teams competed in IP-related exercises.

This approach made the concept of IP more relatable and relevant to the researchers' goals.

As a consequence, the commercialisation arm of the organisation was in a better position to extract previously hidden IP and convert it to revenue – benefiting the organisation as a whole as well as the researchers' careers.

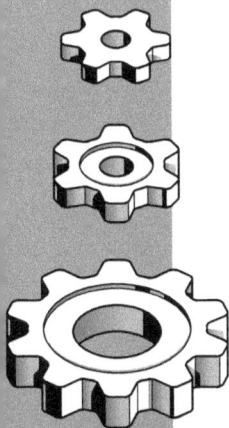

16

EMPLOYEE CONTRACTS

"It is the interactions with others that determine whether intellectual property is diminished or multiplied."

KATE WILSON, IP STRATEGIST

Employees contribute significantly to the intellectual property in a business. They can also easily destroy it. As with any other third-party interactions, a written agreement defines and clarifies expectations.

In many countries, Individual Employment Agreements (IEAs) are a legal requirement. Even where they are not, well-drafted IEAs are highly beneficial as they set clear conditions and expectations, potentially preventing costly misunderstandings.

Ideally, the IP clauses in an IEA (or the company "house rules") should address:

✓ Procedures for identifying and capturing intellectual property

✓ Confidential information and how it is to be handled

✓ A publication policy to prevent valuable IP from being disclosed prematurely to the public or competitors; publication protocols are discussed in greater detail below

✓ A clear documentation policy specifying what should be recorded and how

✓ **A knowledge management system** that distinguishes proprietary or confidential information from general skills and knowledge. This helps avoid disputes about whether an employee used general expertise from previous roles or breached confidentiality by using proprietary information.

Employers should reinforce these expectations through exit interviews, reminding departing employees of their IP obligations. At this stage, it's also essential to obtain signatures on any necessary documents, such as patent and copyright assignments.

Publication Protocols and Researchers

When working with research organisations including universities, I emphasise the importance of publication protocols. These protocols help control the dissemination of information, ensuring that academics receive the recognition they deserve and that organisations can secure the commercial gains necessary to continue their work.

However, enforcing these protocols can be challenging, as many research organisations are filled with independent (aka strong-willed) individuals, who may not be as cooperative as employees in more commercial entities.

Globally, Tech Transfer Offices (TTOs)—the commercialisation arms of research organisations—are often met with suspicion by researchers and are not fully accepted or integrated within the organisation.

Good IP practices (such as publication protocols) are more rigorously followed by commercial entities, but often only sporadically adopted by researchers. This can make it difficult for these diverse organisations to later collaborate effectively to commercialise good research.

Therefore, research organisations that wish to work with more commercial entities need to have a disciplined (yet culturally sensitive) approach to controlling publication.

17

INTERNAL MANUALS AND STANDARD OPERATING PROCEDURES (SOPS)

"Remove all the traffic lights, yellow lines, one-way systems and road markings, and let blissful anarchy prevail. I imagine it would produce a kind of harmony."

SADIE JONES, WRITER AND NOVELIST

Creating internal manuals, standardised templates, and SOPs are cost-effective ways to add substantial value to a business and create valuable intangible assets. The benefits include:

Delivering on brand promise – ensuring consistency and quality across all operations.

Efficient use of time – eliminating the need to recreate documents from scratch.

Succession planning – ensuring critical knowledge isn't locked in the heads of a few key individuals.

Reference material – providing a foundation for training and smooth operations.

Meeting regulatory requirements – this can include internal systems such as meeting ISO standards, compliance with government regulations or meeting product safety standards for key markets.

Fewer mistakes – reducing errors, which in turn saves time and prevents resources from being diverted to problem-solving.

Scalability – making it easier to expand by replicating business processes ("cookie-cutting") into new markets. This is particularly relevant with franchise models, as discussed earlier.

This documentation is best protected by copyright and confidentiality.

SOPs are not the sexiest of assets in a business, and their value in underpinning performance is often overlooked. They should however be treated with at least the same reverence as the more exciting technological innovations and brand presence.

18

INDUSTRIAL ESPIONAGE: LOW- AND HIGH-TECH APPROACHES

While no system is completely foolproof, protecting against industrial espionage involves a mix of both low-tech and high-tech approaches. It's crucial to demonstrate clear efforts in identifying proprietary and valuable information, as well as providing appropriate warnings. This can help establish intent and culpability if espionage occurs, and it can influence the severity of penalties.

Low-Tech Approaches

On-site security

Physical security is the first line of defence. Visitor protocols should require sign-ins that not only cover Health and Safety but also include confidentiality agreements regarding the business's intellectual property.

Restricted access to R&D

Research and development areas should have access restricted to personnel on a need-to-know basis. This helps prevent unauthorised exposure to sensitive information.

Exit interviews

When employees leave the organisation, exit interviews should reinforce their continuing obligations regarding IP, getting outstanding patent and copyright assignments, reminding them of confidentiality agreements and other legal requirements.

High-Tech Approaches

Knowledge management systems

These systems should flag proprietary information and restrict access based on the employee's role and need-to-know basis. Logs should also be maintained to track who accessed sensitive information and when, providing a traceable audit trail.

Cybersecurity measures

Every business should implement robust cybersecurity protocols to protect against hacking and cyber-espionage. Regular updates, encrypted communication, and employee training on data protection are essential to securing valuable information.

A combination of low- and high-tech strategies enable businesses to better safeguard against industrial espionage. . Noting that the Courts consider the conduct of both parties. A business that can demonstrate they value their IP through staking reasonable steps to protect it is looked upon favourably.

A personal experience with industrial espionage follows.

Industrial espionage and time travel

A well-written patent specification takes time to craft. Patent attorneys typically ask for a few weeks to prepare one, depending on their workload. So, you can imagine my surprise when one day, at 2pm, I received a call from a client asking me to draft and file a patent application that very day!

It turned out they had just discovered that one of their top employees was an industrial spy and had leaked their new invention to a competitor.

Fortunately, a few things worked in our favour.

First, the invention was low-tech with a clearly identifiable patentable feature, making it easy to quickly understand and write up.

Second, they had excellent CAD drawings, which provided a solid basis for the application. Even if the written description missed something, the drawings ensured that we had some coverage.

But perhaps the most fortunate factor was that they were based in New Zealand, which operates in the world's most advanced time zone. This allowed us to draft the patent specification and then have an associate on the West Coast of the United States file it within their time zone—securing a priority date the day before the invention was leaked!

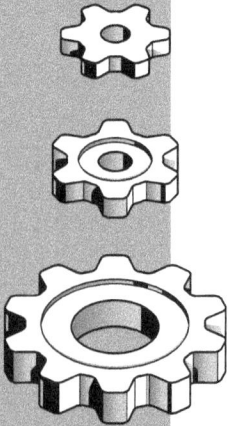

19

CLIENT ONBOARDING PROCEDURES

"A poor onboarding experience is hard to come back from and is the fastest way to lose a customer. It's critical to actively think about the entire customer journey. Define It, Map It, Document It."

PAUL PHILP, CEO OF AMITY

Discussions around intellectual property (IP) can be delicate, especially when raised with existing clients, as they can infer a lack of trust. However, addressing the treatment of IP is crucial for both the organisation and its clients. The best approach is to handle this at the start of a project, presenting it as part of the organisation's standard procedures.

A well-crafted Terms of Engagement (TOE) that addresses IP issues may include the following terms—although each project will require its own tailored considerations:

✓ The organisation retains ownership of all IP generated from the engagement. This ensures control over its use.

✓ The organisation is free to use the IP for other projects. This provides opportunities for scalability.

✓ All information related to the project remains confidential until the organisation indicates otherwise. This allows time to file for valid IP rights or implement other protection measures.

✓ The organisation may use anonymised data for other projects or internal purposes. This helps to identify trends.

While concerns about client pushback are understandable, the onboarding process can actually present a strategic opportunity. One possible approach is to introduce a tiered pricing structure, offering clients varying levels of rights depending on what they are willing to pay for.

Possible scenarios include:

✓ The client pays the base fee, with the organisation retaining all rights and the freedom to produce similar work for the client's competitors.

✓ The client pays a higher fee to prevent the organisation from producing similar work for direct competitors but allows for work in other jurisdictions, potentially placing the organisation on retainer.

✓ The client pays a premium for exclusive rights, preventing the organisation from producing similar work for anyone else, with the organisation retained for future work.

✓ The client pays a substantial premium for exclusive rights, ensuring that no similar work is produced for any other client and without the organisation being placed on retainer.

The final letter of engagement will reflect the terms agreed upon during these discussions.

Be prepared to push the limits of what you have previously considered feasible, and invest in important conversations about the value of IP, client expectations, and what clients are willing to pay for these rights.

20

IP WARNINGS AND MARKETING COLLATERAL

Any non-litigious deterrent or barrier to entry, particularly if inexpensive to implement, should be considered. This is where IP warnings on marketing collateral can be valuable.

Marketing collateral refers to the materials used to support the sales and marketing of a product or service.

Including IP warnings on marketing collateral serves several purposes. It can

✓ deter potential infringers,

✓ showcase valuable IP

✓ enhance the brand's reputation with customers, and

✓ establish a legal trail that could support claims for damages.

The following are recommended IP warnings for the various types of IP.

Trade marks

Whenever a trade mark is used, it should be accompanied by the appropriate symbol—either the ™ symbol (if unregistered) or the ® symbol (if registered). For example: LOGO®.

If there are several trade marks being used, then a footnote can be used instead to save cluttering the collateral. For example, "Hidden Mechanics", Brandstorming", "Three Cogs Formula" and the gear logo are all registered trade marks of KTPI Enterprises Ltd".

Patents, designs, and technology

If the collateral relates to technology that is protected by formal IP rights (such as a patent or design application), this should be mentioned, ideally in a footnote; for instance, "US Patent Appn. No. 123456 & International patent applications pending."

Copyright

All marketing collateral has some form of copyright associated with it. As a general precaution, including fine print at the bottom of each piece of collateral; for example, "© BUSINESS Ltd 2025".

Businesses should review all marketing collateral to ensure that appropriate IP markings are in place, then incorporate these results into their brand guidelines to ensure consistent application across new materials.

21

PREPARATION OF TENDER DOCUMENTS

"Those are the two best words in English, "Bidding" and "war".
EVAN DAUGHERTY, AMERICAN WRITER

In many sectors, especially in public or government procurement, tendering is required to ensure compliance with regulations and standards, as well as provide public confidence in procurement practices. Tendering can provide several benefits, particularly for organisations and businesses seeking to procure goods, services, or works in a transparent and competitive manner.

However, the parties tendering face many potential pitfalls with intellectual property often inadvertently given away.

Tender documents require careful management, as businesses must strike a balance between providing enough information to win the tender and not disclosing so much that a competitor could use it. While there is no exact formula for achieving this balance, several strategies can help protect the IP contained within tender documents, but also swing the balance towards the IP-savvy tenderer.

It is important that the recipients of any tender document understand the value placed on IP by the tenderer, and that they hesitate before considering taking or distributing that IP. One way to achieve this is by prominently highlighting IP rights throughout the document.

Using IP to Swing a Tender

It can be tempting for an organisation to take the best ideas they receive in a tender process and then ask the cheapest tenderer if they can deliver on those ideas—even if another party submitted them.

Therefore, to swing a tender your way, place protective measures around the key "winning" elements. These measures can be patents, confidentiality, or exclusive access to a special resource.

Whatever the protective measure, it can deter an organisation from giving a tender to a party that may infringe on another's rights.

Further, part of the tendering process may be to guarantee exclusive rights (say a licence) to the winning elements, which is achievable only because of the protective measures.

Confidentiality

Even with the best intentions, it is easy for recipients of tender documents to unintentionally breach confidentiality or fail to treat the document with the respect it deserves. While "CONFIDENTIAL" is often placed on the front page of tender documents, it should also appear on subsequent pages—either as a watermark or in the footer. This ensures that, if pages are copied, any additional recipients cannot deny the confidential nature of the material.

Use

Many tender documents include a disclaimer around use, such as: "Intended for use by only the parties named in it." While this is a good start, it can be improved by explicitly stating that the document is confidential and must be treated as such. The parties should be instructed not to disseminate the material, in addition to having the confidentiality footer, as discussed above.

Copyright

Tenderers also need to appreciate that usually they own copyright in all imagery and wording they prepare for their tender documents or presentations. A copyright notice should be placed in the footer of presentation slides or tender images, and copyright should also be referenced in a disclaimer.

Other IP Warnings

Tender documents can also contain additional IP warnings, as discussed in Chapter 20 in relation to marketing collateral to reinforce the value and protection of the material presented.

Highlighting that you have you valuable IP in a tender document can positively bias winning of the tender your way as well as deterring others from capitalising upon your IP.

22

COPYRIGHT

"Only one thing is impossible for God: To find any sense in any copyright law on the planet."

MARK TWAIN, AMERICAN WRITER AND HUMOURIST

Copyright is a unique right that, in most cases, arises automatically upon the creation of a "copyright work". It has broad applicability, covering various forms of creative output including art, music, literature, marketing materials, industrial design, plans, forms, content, packaging, templates, websites, and software.

Coverage

While copyright protects the expression of an idea, it does not cover concepts. For example, someone could reword the concepts in a training manual without infringing copyright, but they would not be able to copy the exact wording or closely mimic the page layout.

Copyright can also cover the likes of source code in software—just the precise code and not the functionality, which could be covered by patents.

Protecting concepts, often the domain of patents, is discussed in the Technology section.

Copyright infringement occurs only if actual copying can be demonstrated. For example, a third party could replicate the functionality of a 3D modelling system without breaching copyright. However, directly copying a significant part of the proprietary software supporting the system may lead to copyright infringement.

It's important to mark copyright notices on all developed copyright works to assert rights clearly.

Ownership

Generally, the original creator is considered the copyright owner. However, if a work is "commissioned"—meaning that another party instructs and pays for the creation of the work—the commissioner can be regarded as the owner.

In most countries, copyright ownership can only be transferred in writing, so it is essential to ensure any agreements related to intellectual property explicitly mention copyright.

I have encountered cases where businesses believed they had purchased all assets, only to discover later that the Sale and Purchase agreement did not include copyright. This often becomes apparent when the new "owner" tries to enforce their rights and finds they have none. Even more problematic is when the original owner has died or is unreachable, making it difficult to assign copyright post-sale.

Ownership can become complicated when a project involves multiple contributors. A good approach is to record each party's contribution to help avoid disputes later. Matters get even murkier when later artists are "inspired" by earlier works.

"Free" Use of External Content

When borrowing content from external sources such as the internet, organisations need to consider copyright. Educational institutions may have limited licences to copy some works, but it's important to follow certain guidelines. In general, external content can be used if:

✓ It is subject to a Creative Commons licence, with proper attribution to the author, or

✓ The copyright has expired, or

✓ Explicit permission has been granted by the copyright owner.

Always seek specific legal advice before proceeding with the use of external copyrighted content.

The laws around copyright are highly subjective, therefore if copyrighted material is what gives you a competitive edge, make sure that you know the "rules" and have good internal systems that provide clarity around scope and ownership of the material.

The "Blurred Lines" case

A notable example of copyright complexity in collaborative works is the famous "Blurred Lines" case, which highlights important aspects of copyright law, particularly in music compositions with multiple contributors.

This involved a lawsuit between the estate of Marvin Gaye, and Pharrell Williams and Robin Thicke, the latter two being the creators of the hit song "Blurred Lines". The lawsuit, filed in 2013, claimed that "Blurred Lines" incorporated elements of Gaye's 1977 song "Got to Give It Up". The key issue in the case was whether the two songs were "substantially similar" in terms of rhythm, melody, and overall feel, rather than direct note-for-note copying.

In 2015, a jury ruled in favour of Marvin Gaye's estate, awarding $7.4 million (later reduced to $5.3 million) in damages. The ruling sparked a heated debate in the music industry. Critics argued it set a dangerous precedent, potentially stifling creativity by making artists fearful of being sued for drawing inspiration from the style or "vibe" of earlier works. The case underscored the complexities of copyright law, especially in the area of music, where influences are often subtle and hard to define.

The verdict was later upheld on appeal in 2018, solidifying its importance in copyright law.

The song "Blurred Lines" also inspired a very clever parody by Auckland Law School. Check it out!

(https://www.youtube.com/watch?v=tC1XtnLRLPM)

Ed Sheeran's Experience

"If we lose our freedom to be inspired, one day we'll find that the entertainment industry has become stuck in a cycle of litigation."
ED SHEERAN, BRITISH SINGER-SONGWRITER, MUSICIAN, AND RECORD PRODUCER

Ed Sheeran has been vocal about the challenges posed by copyright law in the music industry, having faced several lawsuits, including those over "Shape of You" and "Thinking Out Loud". His experience has led him to speak out about the broader implications of these cases.

"Thinking Out Loud" vs. "Let's Get It On"

In 2016, the estate of Ed Townsend, who co-wrote Marvin Gaye's "Let's Get It On", sued Sheeran, claiming that his song, "Thinking Out Loud" (2014), copied the harmonic progression and rhythmic elements of the 1973 classic. The case has centred on whether the two songs' chord progression and overall feel are sufficiently similar to warrant copyright infringement.

Sheeran denied any copying and argued that similar chord progressions are common in pop music, which should not constitute copyright infringement. He won the case in 2023.

"Shape of You" vs. "Oh Why"

In 2018, Sheeran was accused of plagiarising parts of Sami Chokri's song "Oh Why" (2015) for his hit, "Shape of You" (2017). Chokri claimed that Sheeran's hook ("Oh I") was strikingly similar to his own. Sheeran denied the accusations, and in 2022, the High Court in London ruled in Sheeran's favour, stating that there was no evidence he had deliberately copied "Oh Why". The judge concluded that the similarities were "coincidental" and did not amount to copyright infringement.

After winning the case, Sheeran expressed frustration over the increasing number of lawsuits in the music industry, describing them as baseless attempts to profit from successful artists.

These cases highlight ongoing challenges in music copyright law, where questions about the boundaries of inspiration, common chord progressions, and originality frequently arise.

23

COPYRIGHT IN REWRITTEN MATERIAL

When I asked ChatGPT who would own copyright if I asked it to rewrite some text, the response was as follows:

> "The rewritten material, produced as a result of our interaction, would still belong to you. As the original creator and because you're commissioning the rewrite by submitting your text for modification, the copyright of the revised content remains with you. My role is to assist in refining and enhancing your original work based on your input, not to claim ownership of it."
>
> *ChatGPT*

I thought that this was very magnanimous of ChatGPT, and somewhat out of sync with interpretation of copyright law when a human contributes to revision of copyright material. This applies not only to works of literature but also to software, graphics, music and the creation of marketing collateral for businesses.

The question of whether an editor can claim copyright over an author's material is a nuanced one, depending on the nature of the editor's contributions and the legal jurisdiction in question. Copyright generally vests in the person who creates an original work, but an editor's role can sometimes "blur the lines" (see what I did there?). Currently, a book written by AI exclusively is thought to have no copyright associated with it.

In general, editing does not automatically grant copyright ownership to an editor. Copyright remains with the author unless the editor makes significant, creative contributions that meet the threshold for copyright protection. Even in such cases, the editor's rights will likely extend only to their additions or changes, not to the original work. Contractual agreements and the nature of the relationship between author and editor play a crucial role in determining copyright claims. Therefore, it's essential for both authors and editors to clearly outline their rights and expectations in written contracts to avoid disputes.

Here's a breakdown of key considerations:

Original Authorship
The mere act of editing someone else's work does not inherently give the editor copyright if the editor is simply making routine corrections, such as fixing grammar, punctuation, or spelling errors. These changes are not considered "original" or "creative" enough to qualify for copyright protection.

Substantial Contribution
To claim copyright, an editor must contribute original material that transforms the work in a substantial and creative way. This could occur in instances where the editor significantly reshapes the material—adding new ideas, rewriting sections, or even restructuring the work in a way that requires substantial creativity. In such cases, the editor's contribution could be seen as co-authorship or the creation of a derivative work, which may entitle the editor to some copyright interest in the edited version.

However, the editor would still not hold copyright over the original material created by the author. Instead, they would have rights only over the elements they contributed.

This principle also applies when a "work" is a combination of human and AI contributions.

Employment or Contractual Agreements
The question of who holds copyright can also depend on the nature of the relationship between the creator and the reviser. If, in relation to book creation, the editor is working under an employment contract or as part of a publisher's editorial team, any changes or contributions they make are often considered "works made for hire". In these cases, the copyright in any editorial contributions typically belongs to the employer or the contracting party, not the individual editor.

Similarly, if the editor is hired as a freelancer, the terms of their contract will determine whether they have any claim to copyright. Most freelance agreements will specify that all rights, including any creative contributions, belong to the author or publisher.

Joint Authorship

If the author and editor work closely together to co-create the final piece, and if both parties intend that the work be considered a joint effort, then the editor might have a claim as a co-author. In this case, the editor and author would share copyright ownership. However, this is relatively rare in the context of editing. It is more common in collaborative projects, where both parties contribute significant creative input.

Moral Rights

While editors may not always have copyright claims, they could seek recognition through moral rights, which protect the editor's right to be acknowledged for their contributions. In some jurisdictions, these moral rights allow an editor to assert that their contributions have added creative value, though this doesn't equate to full copyright ownership.

Derivative Works

If the editor makes enough changes that the edited work qualifies as a derivative work, the editor could hold copyright in the new version, but not the original text. A derivative work is a version of the original that has been altered, adapted, or transformed significantly. The editor's copyright would cover only their specific contributions, not the original work itself, which remains under the author's copyright.

Overall, the terms of a relationship that a creator has with any third party (such as an editor) needs to be defined at the start of the relationship and reference intellectual property considerations.

24

PARODIES – COPYRIGHT LAW SANCTIONING HUMOUR

Parodies often fall under a fair use doctrine, which exempts them from copyright infringement in many countries.

Creating a parody while avoiding copyright infringement involves navigating both legal and creative boundaries. In the UK, copyright law allows for certain uses of protected works without permission, provided they fall under "fair dealing" exceptions, which is called fair use in the US. Parody is one such exception, but there are specific rules to follow.

"Weird Al" Yankovic is an American singer widely known for his humorous and clever parodies of popular songs, and his approach to creating parodies—a prime example of how to respect copyright laws—is discussed below.

Seeking Permission

While Yankovic is not legally required to obtain permission under US law, he consistently seeks permission from the original artists before releasing his parodies. This is not a legal necessity but a personal and professional decision. Yankovic has said that this practice helps maintain good relationships within the music industry, and, in some cases, artists have appreciated the gesture. For instance, Michael Jackson was a major supporter, allowing Yankovic to parody both "Beat It" and "Bad".

Transformative Element

The parody should add something new, offering commentary, criticism, or humour, rather than simply copying the original. The intent is to mock or satirise the original work, or a societal issue, without replicating it in full.

Yankovic's parodies are often highly transformative, which is key to avoiding copyright infringement. He uses the melody and rhythm of well-known songs but entirely changes the lyrics to offer humorous commentary or create absurd scenarios. For instance, his parody of "Smells Like Teen Spirit" by Nirvana, titled "Smells Like Nirvana", pokes fun at the unintelligibility of the original song's lyrics. This transformation from serious grunge music to light-hearted commentary is a perfect example of how parody adds something new to the original.

Fair Dealing

The amount of the original work used must be reasonable and appropriate for the purpose. You cannot take more than necessary. This ensures that the parody doesn't harm the original work's market value or exploit the original for commercial gain.

No Confusion

A parody must not cause confusion about its connection to the original. It should be clear that the parody is a separate work, created with a distinct purpose.

Yankovic's parodies exist alongside the original songs without negatively affecting their market value. In fact, they often bring renewed attention to the original work. Parody, by nature, should not be a substitute for the original; instead, it should stand on its own with a different intent and audience. His work illustrates how parody can thrive without detracting from the original artist's success.

His fans know that his versions are distinct comedic interpretations, ensuring no one is misled into thinking they are buying the original.

No Defamation

While parody often involves critique, it must not cross the line into defamatory statements that could harm the reputation of the original creator or work.

By following these principles, creators can craft parodies that respect the balance between creative freedom and the protection of intellectual property rights.

Yankovic's humour is playful and rarely intended to be derogatory or mean-spirited. This has helped him avoid controversy and legal disputes. Artists often find his parodies flattering, as they highlight the cultural relevance of their original songs. For instance, "Amish Paradise", a parody of Coolio's "Gangsta's Paradise", is funny without insulting the original song or artist, even though there was initially a misunderstanding about Coolio's consent.

By following these principles, Yankovic has enjoyed a long career as a parody artist, all while maintaining the respect of fellow musicians and adhering to legal standards regarding copyright.

Yankovic's approach serves as a model for how to create transformative works that honour both creative freedom and intellectual property. Be like Al.

25

TIMING AND SPRINGBOARDS

"You don't have to swing hard to hit a home run. If you got the timing, it'll go."
YOGI BERRA, AMERICAN BASEBALL PLAYER, AND GENERATOR OF SOME OF THE BEST QUOTES EVER!

When crafting an IP strategy, an appreciation of timing helps. Particularly relevant to I-Stuff is understanding the research and development effort required to bring a project to commercial fruition, and how long it could take for others to compete if there were no formal barriers to entry such as patents, and only confidentiality.

Generally, the longer it would take for a competitor to catch up is proportional to the value of the know-how and other intangible assets that contribute to the project. In particular, the contribution of key people such as lead researchers can be better appreciated.

From this, strategies can be put into place to protect the I-stuff which consider other milestones such as product launch, and timing of expenditure on IP protection.

This information is also useful if key personnel leave and misappropriate their previous employer's know-how. Many legal systems recognise the adverse commercial impact which this can cause, and one of the mechanisms by which this can be redressed is through a springboard injunction.

A springboard injunction is a legal remedy designed to prevent a party from gaining an unfair competitive advantage due to their misuse of confidential information or breach of duty. Unlike traditional injunctions that focus on the protection of information itself, a springboard injunction focuses on neutralising the unfair advantage gained from improper actions.

A springboard injunction can achieve the following:

✓ Deprive the wrongdoer of an "unfair head start" obtained through illicit use of confidential data or breach of contract

✓ Restrain the beneficiary of any unfair advantage from capitalising on it for a specified period, rather than indefinitely

✓ Injunct for the time it would have taken the wrongdoer to achieve the advantage legitimately, had they not engaged in misconduct.

The remedy serves as a balance between enforcing fair competition and ensuring the wrongdoer does not profit from unethical practices.

Often an IP strategy recommends identifying proprietary knowledge and safeguarding it with strong internal systems, controlling access to sensitive information, and managing third-party relationships through contracts. This may lessen the chances of a springboard injunction being required and/or provide evidence required to support the injunction.

26

NEGATIVE KNOW-HOW

"One of the more interesting IP concepts is negative know-how—recognising that even mistakes can be valuable!"
KATE WILSON, IP STRATEGIST

It is rare in Research & Development (R&D) for the perfect solution to pop up first time. If it did, the solution probably would not be considered inventive, and thus not patentable. Instead, in R&D, many dead-end paths are taken before a commercially viable solution is found.

These dead-end paths (aka negative know-how) can be valuable in their own right—and not just for supporting inventiveness in a patent specification (discussed in Chapter 28 Sweet Spots).

An example of how negative know-how can be translated into tangible value comes from an organisation I know which uses their understanding of intangible assets to rescue failing businesses.

In this case, their client was a research company in serious financial trouble. Fortunately, the company kept lab books which held details of "failed" research. These lab books ended up being sold to a competitor of the research company—which saved the purchaser from going down wrong research paths. The result was that the value of the sale of this "negative know-how" was enough to rescue their client!

Documentation and confidentiality protocols which often form part of the recommendations in an IP strategy help capture valuable know-how.

Next, we look at the more readily protectable Quarter of competitive edge: technology.

QUARTER 3
TECHNOLOGY

"A country without a patent office and good patent laws was just a crab and couldn't travel any way but sideways or backwards."

MARK TWAIN, AMERICAN WRITER AND HUMOURIST

I am a tech enthusiast with a passion for innovation, especially when it comes to new technologies. As a patent attorney with a background in science, drafting patents for inventions was my first love in the intellectual property field. The excitement of learning something entirely new each day was what motivated me to head into work with enthusiasm.

Inventions have transformed our lives, and their contributions to the world are immeasurable. The original patent system was established to encourage travellers to explore abroad and bring back innovations to their home country. In return for the risk and expense, they were rewarded with a Crown-granted monopoly (a patent) to commercialise their discoveries locally before the innovation eventually entered the public domain to benefit the wider population.

Today, many businesses are hesitant to embark on the innovation journey unless they have a means of protecting their efforts. R&D costs must be recouped and are factored into the pricing of the final product. If a competitor can copy the product without investing in the same R&D, then they can undercut the original creator by pricing their product lower—a situation that hardly seems fair!

The following graph highlights a typical breakdown of costs that contribute to a product's final price. While these figures may vary by industry, an average contribution of 20% R&D is often a reasonable estimate. Factoring in the usual mark-up from manufacturer to warehouse to retailer, the dollar difference can be significant between the more expensive original trying to recoup R&D costs and the copier piggybacking on their innovation coattails with a cut-price equivalent.

This is where patents come into play. For a limited period (usually up to 20 years), the innovator enjoys a monopoly, allowing them to recoup their R&D and other investments by preventing competitors from copying their work. The monopoly granted to a patentee is significant, providing exclusive rights to make, sell, license, use, import, and export the invention as defined in the patent claims, within the country where the patent is granted.

Comparison of Price Points - with and without R&D

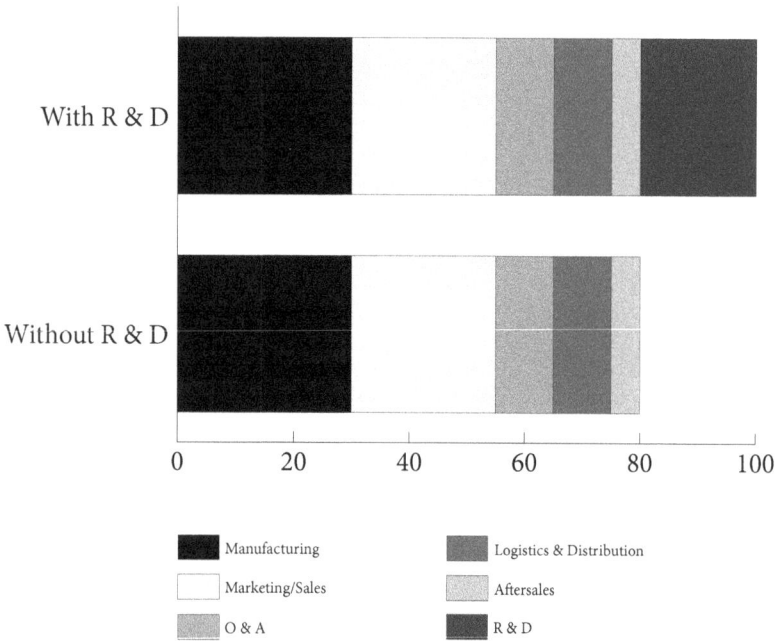

	Manufacturing		Logistics & Distribution
	Marketing/Sales		Aftersales
	O & A		R & D

In addition to patents, trade secrets offer a means to maintain a competitive edge by protecting improvements in functionality. Meanwhile, open-source strategies, although they do not offer competitive protection, can facilitate the rapid adoption of foundational technologies.

This section explores all these approaches, but with a particular emphasis on patents.

27

WHAT IS PATENTABLE?

"I don't think necessity is the mother of invention.
Invention, in my opinion, arises directly from idleness,
possibly also from laziness, to save oneself the trouble."
DAME AGATHA CHRISTIE, QUEEN OF CRIME®

More can be patented than most realise—the general criterion being that the "invention" to be patented must be novel and inventive as well as being of patentable subject matter.

The rules around patentability differ per country, which can trip businesses up when they are expanding into unfamiliar territories. Rely upon your IP advisor to guide you as to what rights you can get before committing to an export country.

Patentable Subject Matter

Patent law and its interpretation is continually evolving. In general, what can be considered patentable is narrowing as case law refines understanding of the intention of the law and the consequent impact on novelty and inventiveness of prior art. At one stage, business plans were considered patentable, but not now. Software often needs to meet certain criteria to be considered patentable. Morality clauses in some countries prevent methods of medical treatment to humans (and sometimes animals).

A business can use knowledge of where patent protection can be gained (or not) for their product to guide their R&D efforts and market choices.

This table summarises the different types of patentable subject matter and their general eligibility in selected jurisdictions.

PATENTABLE SUBJECT MATTER	DESCRIPTION	NZ	UK/EU	US	AU	CN	IN
Products (Devices, Compositions)	Mechanical tools, electronic devices, chemicals, pharmaceuticals	✓	✓	✓	✓	✓	✓
Manufacturing Processes	Methods for producing goods or materials	✓	✓	✓	✓	✓	✓
Chemical/ Biological Processes	Synthesis, fermentation, purification	✓	✓	✓	✓	✓	✓
Software-related Inventions	If providing a technical effect (e.g., image compression)	!*	!*	✓	✓	!	!
Medical Devices	Surgical tools, implants, diagnostic apparatus	✓	✓	✓	✓	✓	✓
Medical Treatment Methods	Direct methods for treatment or diagnosis on humans	✗	✗	✓	✓	✗	✗
New Use of Known Substances	e.g., aspirin for heart health	✓	✓	✓	✓	✓	✓
Microorganisms	Engineered bacteria, yeasts (must be described or deposited)	✓	✓	✓	✓	✓	!
Business Methods	Only if involving technical innovation	!	✗	!	!	✗	✗
Plant Varieties / Animal Breeds	Whole breeds or varieties	✗	✗	✓†	✗	✗	✗
Genes and Traits (Modified)	Genetic modifications or specific trait patents	✓	✓	✓	✓	!	✗
Combinations / Systems	Novel integrations of components	✓	✓	✓	✓	✓	✓

Legend:

✓ = Generally patentable   ✗ = Generally not patentable

! = Restricted/patentable only in specific circumstances

✓† = Subject to moral exclusions; e.g., cloning or human embryos

Novelty

To be novel, an invention must have a feature (or combination of features) that is different from anything that is already known. In patent attorney jargon, what is already known is called prior art—which can include written publications, physical demonstrations, online presence, and working the invention for commercial gain.

In most countries, a patent application must be filed before there is public disclosure of an invention. Therefore, a standard recommendation is that before a patent application is filed, all discussions about an invention are held in confidence, preferably with a signed confidentiality agreement. Otherwise, you could sabotage potential patentability of your invention by being your own prior art.

However, there are some novelty exceptions such as grace periods. Included in the list of countries having these are the United States, Australia and New Zealand. Grace periods allow inventors to publicly disclose an invention without losing the right to patent, under certain conditions.

Another novelty condition that is less well known is that an offer for sale can destroy novelty, even if the discussions are held in confidence.

There are also other novelty exceptions, so if there is a premature disclosure, check with your IP specialist as to whether your potential patent protection can be rescued.

Inventiveness

An invention must involve an inventive step to be patentable, meaning it must not be obvious to a person "skilled in the art". This is a very subjective judgement and not only varies per country, but can also vary between individual patent examiners in a Patent Office.

My take on inventiveness is to find a novel feature and then see if there is a story behind it that shows that that the feature provides an advantage (generally commercial) over the prior art. The "story", as such, needs to show some of the hardship undertaken to find a solution or improvement.

The concept of inventiveness is discussed more in the Anatomy of a Patent Specification section, but a special type of invention (sweet spots) and how to showcase their inventiveness is discussed next.

Understanding the patentability criteria of novelty, inventiveness and subject matter, is essential to implementing systems that preserve the protectability of the competitive edge given by technological advancements.

28

SWEET SPOTS

"The magic happens when you find the sweet spot where your genuine interests, skills, and opportunity intersect."

SCOTT BELSKY, AMERICAN ENTREPRENEUR AND WRITER

Sometimes it is worth patenting an incremental improvement; that is, finding a sweet spot. Patents for sweet spots, more formally known as selection inventions, can be powerful if the sweet spot represents the most commercially valuable form of an invention.

Selection invention patents are particularly useful if a product has to meet regulatory considerations such as Food and Drug Administration (FDA) approval. Obtaining FDA (or equivalent) approval is generally an expensive and time-consuming exercise requiring submission of clinical trial results.

A savvy operator will file for patent protection with narrow claims matching that of the FDA submission. Often, narrower claims can be easier and cheaper to obtain than broader ones due to there being fewer ~~arguments~~ discussions with patent examiners.

A patent with claims matching regulatory approval acts as a significant barrier to entry to a competitor. If the competitor wants to market a similar product, then the competitor will also need to gain regulatory approval. The cheapest way to do this is to effectively piggyback on the original registration by showing that its product is the same as the one that is already registered. However, if this is done, then the competitor infringes the patent!

If a competitor then tries to design outside the claims of the narrow patent, the competitor will have to go through an expensive regulatory process for its non-infringing product, thus making it less competitive because of having to recoup trial costs in its pricing.

However, to get a selection invention patent, the hurdle of inventiveness must be overcome. This requires data supporting that the sweet spot has significant advantages and that the range that defines the sweet spot was not an obvious one to choose. This includes keeping records of experiments that didn't work – aka Negative Know-how.

An IP strategist who has input into the experimental design can give guidance as to what data will provide the best support for selection invention patent claims. This can mitigate the frustrating situation of asking a patent attorney to draft a patent specification, only to be told to go back and get more data!

29

NOTABLE PATENTED INVENTIONS

Can you imagine a world without some of these groundbreaking patented inventions? Note that all images are derived from the actual patent drawings.

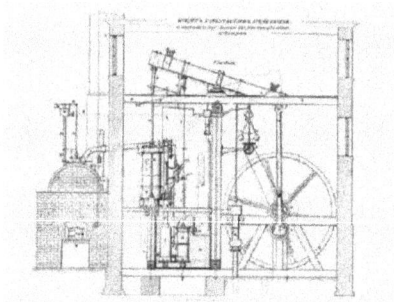

Steam engine improvements (James Watt, 1769)

Watt's inventions, including the separate condenser, drastically improved the efficiency of steam engines and were a driving force behind the Industrial Revolution.

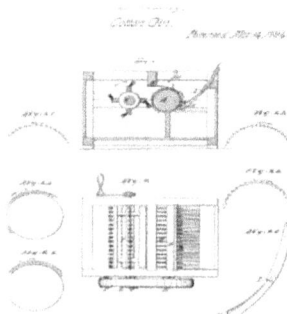

Cotton gin (Eli Whitney, 1794)

This invention revolutionised the cotton industry by vastly speeding up the process of separating cotton fibres from seeds.

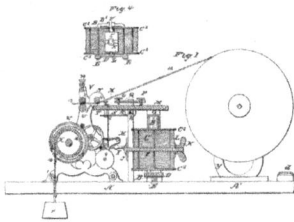

Telegraph (Samuel Morse, 1837)

The electric telegraph changed communication forever, allowing instant messages to be sent over long distances.

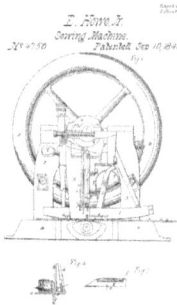

Sewing machine (Elias Howe, 1846)

Howe's invention greatly increased garment production efficiency, accelerating the growth of the textile industry.

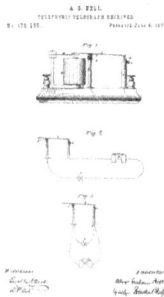

Telephone (Alexander Graham Bell, 1876)

Bell's telephone transformed communication, enabling voice conversations over great distances.

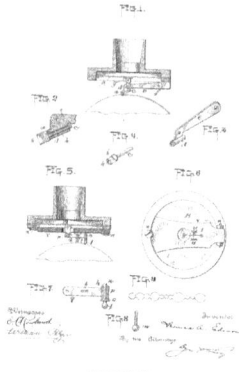

Phonograph (Thomas Edison, 1877)

The phonograph was the first device able to record and reproduce sound, paving the way for the music and entertainment industries.

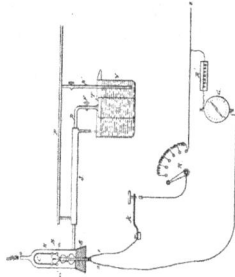

Light bulb (Thomas Edison, 1880)

Edison's improvements to the light bulb made it practical for everyday use, lighting homes and cities across the world.

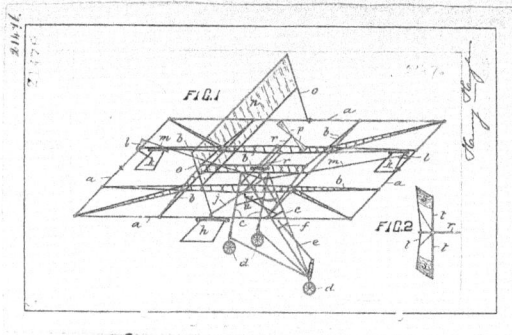

Flying machine (Richard Pearse, 1902)

This New Zealand inventor pre-dated the Wright brothers' flying machine, whose later flight marked the dawn of aviation with controlled, powered flight. Being proud Kiwis (New Zealanders), we gave this patent drawing pride of place in our offices. Ironic that the kiwi, our native bird, is flightless…

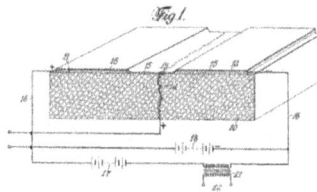

Transistor (John Bardeen, Walter Brattain, and William Shockley, 1947)

The invention of the transistor revolutionised electronics and computing, forming the basis of almost all modern electronic devices.

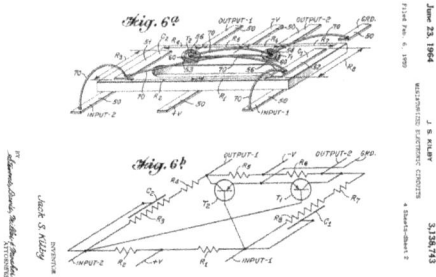

Integrated circuit (Jack Kilby and Robert Noyce, 1959)

This groundbreaking invention laid the foundation for the computer and electronics industries we know today.

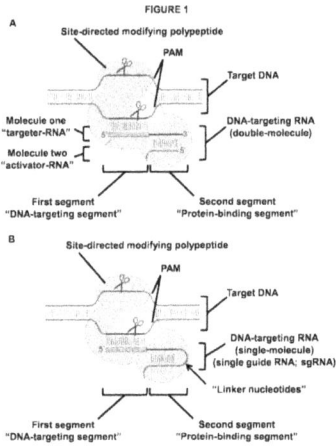

FIGURE 1

CRISPR-Cas9 gene editing
(Jennifer Doudna and Emmanuelle Charpentier, 2012)

This technology has revolutionised genetics, offering precise DNA editing with vast implications for medicine, agriculture, and biotechnology.

30

MORE THAN JUST A LEGAL DOCUMENT

"I make more mistakes than anyone else I know, and sooner or later, I patent most of them."

THOMAS EDISON, INVENTOR WITH 2,332 PATENTS

Those new to the innovation industry can ofttimes think that just gaining a patent for their invention will set them up for success. But a patent is a business tool, not a "tick the box" legal document or the holy grail to riches.

An analytical approach is needed to look at what the business is trying to achieve and how or if a patent can help that. This needs to be understood by both the patent attorney and the patentee.

Amongst the considerations are budget, timing and resource. While a patent attorney can craft the ultimate patent specification, practically it will be tempered by these considerations.

Clear communication between the patent attorney and patentee about the purpose of the patent before drafting is critical. The following are some of the reasons a business may wish to obtain a patent, along with how the patent specification can be drafted to support those aims as well as showcasing the invention to other parties.

Attracting Investors

Ideally, the patentee has researched likely investors they wish to target (Competitive Intelligence in the next Section). The general description in the patent specification can then include an example or two of how the invention can be used in a field that the investor is interested in—hopefully, encouraging investment!

Deterrent to Competitors

Sometimes a business needs time to gain traction in the marketplace. A broadly drafted patent specification can function as a deterrent causing hesitancy in competitors until the final form of the patent claims are real-

ised. A "Cause to Pause" can be the key to market dominance by the patentee, particularly where the invention is in a niche market or AI/data based.

Controlling Manufacturers

Patents are an excellent tool to control manufacturers of a product, particularly when manufacture is offshore and "over-runs" are viewed as a legitimate way for locals in the country of manufacture to profit. Including
manufacturing guidelines in the patent specification can reinforce a relationship with a manufacturer—noting that manufacturing agreements can
reference patents.

Leverage for Negotiations

Sometimes collaboration with other parties is required to fully commercialise an invention. The general description and possibly some of the
claims can include examples of how the invention can be integrated into
other technologies and/or processes.

Licensing to Get Royalties

The value of an invention can be worth proportionally far more than its
price. A small component in a greater system can be the element that gives
the competitive edge. Patent claims can be crafted not only for the core invention, but for the greater technology into which it is incorporated. While
there are "rules" around how broad you can go, it does not hurt to try.

Royalties can be negotiated for the bigger use of an invention more easily
if the bigger picture is reflected in the patent specification.

Property for Sale

Similar considerations around drafting for investors also apply for pur-
chasers. A difference can be to view where the patent can fit within a greater
portfolio. Often the range of technologies and timings of patents filed within a portfolio can paint a picture of the value of a purchase.

Litigation against Infringers

For many, litigation is the last resort—stressful, expensive and time-consuming. For some, litigation is the business model, rather than building
up a business that manufactures and sells an invention. These businesses
are sometimes kindly referred to as non-practising entities (NPEs) or, less
kindly, as patent trolls.

Therefore, the patent specification can be directed to more speculative inventions designed to block others and extract punitive remedies.

Escrow to Secure Ideas

A Patent Office is an independent body where information in the form of a patent specification can be date-stamped and stored.

This facility can be used to essentially dump information prior to meeting with an outside party. Therefore, if there was a dispute over who contributed what, the Patent Office record can be used to resolve matters.

In this case, the patent attorney probably does not need to craft a patent specification to usual standards and just facilitate the filing of pure information.

Apply an analytical approach to understand what your business is trying to achieve and how or if a patent can help that. Discuss this with your patent attorney so that any patent specification drafted is fit for purpose.

31

ANATOMY OF A PATENT SPECIFICATION

"We think we have solved the mystery of creation. Maybe we should patent the universe and charge everyone royalties for their existence."

STEPHEN HAWKING, WILD WHEELCHAIR DRIVER AND
ENGLISH THEORETICAL PHYSICIST

I have experienced considerable professional frustration over the years trying to salvage "self-drafted" patent specifications.

Discouraging businesses from drafting their own patent specifications is not about being protectionist. While individuals can attempt it, I would recommend it only as a last resort (or perhaps as an escrow tactic, as discussed in Chapter 30), and not because it will provide any meaningful legal protection. Essentially, if an invention holds potential value, it is best to go the professional route.

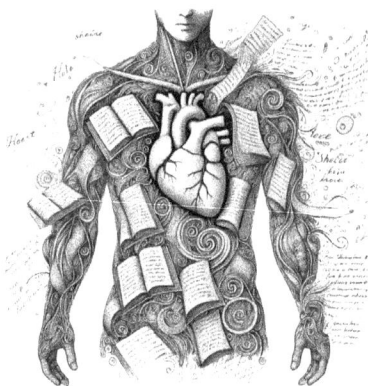

That said, it is still beneficial for inventors and businesses to understand the anatomy of a patent specification, the bones of which are below.

Title – More Than Just a Line

One of the first elements to consider is the title, which can have a surprisingly significant impact on patent rights.

When a patent application is filed, the patent specification remains unpublished, but the title does not. A common mistake is to be overly specific with the title, effectively identifying the invention too early.

This can be very limiting. Patent law requires an invention to be novel when the patent application is filed, and the filing date is critical. Sometimes, you may want to shift the filing date as you are not ready to continue with a patent application. If a descriptive title identifies the invention and is published before the official filing date, it could prevent future patent rights due to lack of novelty. Furthermore, a specific title can narrow the interpretation of the patent's scope.

How does this work in practice?

Imagine you're the first person to invent a retractable ballpoint pen. The wrong title would be

"A Ballpoint Pen with a Click Retraction Mechanism".

This title:

✓ Discloses to competitors what you're working on
✓ Restricts the invention to ballpoint pens, even though the technology could apply to other writing instruments like pencils, felt pens, and crayons
✓ Risks losing novelty if the patent application date shifts
✓ Makes it difficult to cover other retraction mechanisms such as twist or slide.

A better title might be "Apparatus and Method for Operating a Marking Device."

While a patent examiner might find this vague, it is a legitimate title that avoids the issues outlined above.

Field of Invention

This is a brief section that signals the potential applications of the invention. The risk for inexperienced drafters is being too specific, which can limit broader applications.

Background to the Invention – Dissing the Competition?

Patent applicants are required to disclose the closest prior art known to them. This is a legal requirement, but it also helps patent examiners and courts assess the novelty and inventiveness of the invention, which are the key criteria for patentability.

The background section of a patent specification discusses relevant prior art, which may include earlier patents, the applicant's own inventions, competitor products and other publications. This information is gathered through research, aka Competitive Intelligence—the second **Cog** in the **Hidden Mechanics**.

A well-written background section can pre-empt examiner objections (saving considerable attorney costs), help secure a patent and provide a solid foundation for showcasing the invention to investors and other stakeholders.

When explaining this to clients, I often use hand gestures to illustrate how a well-structured discussion strengthens the concept of inventive step which is needed to gain a granted patent. Noting that inventiveness is a highly abstract and subjective concept to grasp and convey.

By focusing on the shortcomings of prior art (flat left hand held low) and then highlighting the improvements introduced by the invention (flat right hand held high), the difference between the two represents the inventive step.

Statement of Invention – The Essence of the Invention

The Statement of Invention (SOI) is the most challenging part of a patent specification to draft. It is a single sentence that captures the essence of the invention and serves as the foundation for the most important patent claim. The SOI also sets the tone for the entire patent specification and is the first part of a patent specification that a patent attorney drafts.

Every word in an SOI is carefully considered. A misplaced word or an unnecessary one could lead to significant financial loss in a patent infringement case.

The Goldilocks zone of patent drafting strikes a balance between being broad enough to cover commercial opportunities and narrow enough to be valid. It should clearly define the key difference between the invention and what already exists. Unless the patent is solely for deterrent purposes, that difference should provide a competitive advantage.

Crafting a strong SOI is one of the most difficult skills for a patent attorney, and it can often be undermined by the business's actions.

To create a robust SOI, the patent attorney must:

- ✓ Know relevant prior art (through Competitive Intelligence). This helps distinguish what the patentee's invention offers that is new and worth patenting. Unfortunately, businesses sometimes publish their ideas prematurely, limiting the eventual scope of protection.

- ✓ Identify the key novel improvements invented. This can take some digging, as inventors often don't realise how inventive their ideas truly are. A patent attorney asking "dumb" questions can help extract key inventive features.

- ✓ Rank these improvements by their commercial significance. This can be tricky without market validation (part of Competitive Intelligence), but paradoxically, validating the market can result in prior publication that could invalidate the patent.

- ✓ Pick the most important improvement to feature in the SOI.

- ✓ Draft the SOI.

- ✓ Explore how competitors might circumvent the SOI, ensuring it's robust.

- ✓ Consider how technology might evolve over the patent's 20-year lifespan, ensuring the language used is future-proof. This also opens the business's mind to possibilities beyond their initial concept.

- ✓ Then, draft the full patent specification in such a way that the SOI is fully supported.

This careful, strategic approach is what gives a patent specification its value and strength.

General Description – Covering the Possibilities

A patent can last for 20 years, which is a long time in the innovation sphere. Consider how technology has evolved over the past two decades.

Ideally, a patent remains relevant throughout its term and deters potential infringers. Thus, it should be crafted to anticipate technological changes over the next 20 years and how these might apply to the core of the invention.

This section of the patent specification outlines the central invention, potential variations, and applications.

Best Method of Performing the Invention – The Nitty Gritty

This is the simplest part of the patent specification to draft. It provides a detailed description of the invention and how it functions, often with reference to technical drawings. The description must be "enabling", meaning it contains enough information for someone skilled in the relevant field to reproduce the invention with relative ease.

Consider whether there are aspects of the technology which are not needed in the patent specification and that could be kept a trade secret, thus adding layers to IP protection.

Claims – Raison d'être

The primary purpose of a patent specification is to support the patent claims, otherwise termed as providing "fair basis".

Patent claims are the statements defining the invention, central to determining patent infringement, and are contested in Patent Offices and Courts worldwide. There are two main types of claims—independent and dependent—along with a raft of special technical claims that I won't bore you with.

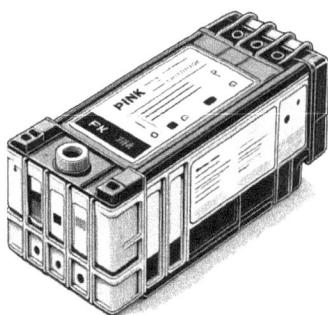

An independent claim stands alone, much like the Statement of Invention, and consists of a single sentence that captures the invention's essence, regardless of whether it is a product or a method.

Dependent claims, however, refer back to other claims. When reading a dependent claim, it is necessary to combine it with the referenced claims for a complete understanding.

Here is an example of an independent claim from HP's first printer inkjet cartridge patent:

1. *An ink jet cartridge for mounting in an ink jet printer, said ink jet cartridge comprising:*

    a housing;

    a jet plate comprising ink ejection nozzles mounted to said housing;

a memory mounted to said housing, wherein said memory stores data related to the types of printers with which the ink jet cartridge can operate.

This claim does not reference other claims, making it clearly independent. Being the first claim also indicates its independence. This claim is short, with few features (referred to as integers in patent terminology), suggesting a broad scope. Since the patent has been granted, the claim is powerful.

Why? Because to infringe a claim, each integer must be present in the infringing product. To avoid infringement, omitting just one essential integer may be enough. Therefore, an ink jet cartridge without a memory mounted to its housing is unlikely to infringe the patent. However, that ink cartridge is unlikely to be as commercially successful as the one claimed in the patent.

HP's fourth claim in the same patent is a dependent claim referencing Claim 1, reading as follows:

4. *The inkjet cartridge of claim 1, wherein said memory comprises an EEPROM.*

To infringe this particular claim, an inkjet cartridge must have all features of Claim 1, combined with the EEPROM memory specified in Claim 4.

Why use dependent claims when independent claims are so strong? Because they serve as an effective fallback. Any claim may be challenged or invalidated, especially if it is found to cover technology existing prior to the patent application. If an independent claim is invalidated, a narrower dependent claim combined with the independent claim may still hold validity.

Further, greater damages can be awarded to patentee if an infringer has been found to infringe multiple patent claims.

Speaking of infringement…

32

PATENT INFRINGEMENT PENALTIES

"Discourage litigation. Persuade your neighbors to compromise whenever you can.... As a peacemaker the lawyer has a superior opportunity of being a good man. There will still be business enough."

ABRAHAM LINCOLN, LAWYER AND 16TH PRESIDENT OF THE UNITED STATES,

As with all IP rights, patents confer a significant monopoly and should be respected.

A notable example of damages awarded in a patent dispute is Monsanto vs. DuPont, which concerned Monsanto's patented Roundup® Ready soybean technology. In 2013, DuPont agreed to pay Monsanto US$1.75 billion over several years to resolve the dispute.

Penalties for patent infringement vary widely across jurisdictions but generally aim to compensate the patent holder for unauthorised use of their invention and discourage future infringements.

Below is an outline of typical penalties:

Monetary Damages

The most common penalty requires the infringer to compensate the patent holder financially. This may include:

- ✓ Compensatory damages: To reimburse the patent holder for lost profits or royalties they would have earned without the infringement.
- ✓ Reasonable royalty: An amount reflecting a reasonable royalty for using the patented technology.
- ✓ Increased damages: In cases of wilful infringement, some jurisdictions (such as the United States) allow courts to increase damages up to three times the assessed amount.

Injunctions

Courts may issue an injunction to prevent further infringement, potentially halting the production, use, sale, or importation of infringing products.

Attorney's Fees and Costs

In specific cases, the infringer may be liable for the patent holder's legal costs.

Destruction or Recall

The infringer may be ordered to destroy or recall infringing products. One of our more memorable cases involved us bashing with a hammer a large number of counterfeit sunglasses which had been delivered to us for destruction. This was actually a case of trade mark and copyright infringement—but the destruction aspect was the same!

Criminal Penalties

Although less common, some jurisdictions impose criminal penalties, including fines and imprisonment, for patent infringement, particularly with counterfeit products.

Border Measures

Customs authorities in some countries may seize infringing goods at the border to block importation under a patent holder's rights.

The enforcement and specifics of these penalties vary based on several factors, including the nature of the infringement, the jurisdiction of the patent, and whether the infringement was wilful or unintentional. Patent law is complex, with outcomes often influenced by numerous legal nuances.

A particularly nuanced form of patent infringement is contributary infringement.

Conducting Freedom to Operate searching before entering a market and getting good advice on the results can mitigate what can be significant legal penalties from patent infringement.

33

CONTRIBUTORY INFRINGEMENT

"Napster's only alleged liability is for contributory or vicarious infringement. So, when Napster's users engage in non-commercial sharing of music, is that activity copyright infringement? No."

DAVID BOIES, AMERICAN LITIGATOR

Contributory infringement is a concept that goes across many types of IP.

The Napster case (referenced above) was a landmark copyright infringement lawsuit in the early 2000s that reshaped the music industry. Napster, a peer-to-peer file-sharing service launched in 1999, allowed users to share and download MP3 music files for free. Major record labels sued Napster in 2000, alleging that it facilitated widespread copyright infringement.

Napster was held liable for contributory and vicarious infringement, as it knowingly enabled users to share copyrighted music without authorisation and had the ability to control that activity. The court ordered Napster to shut down its service unless it could prevent infringing activity, which it failed to do. Napster ultimately ceased operations and filed for bankruptcy in 2002.

Referencing patent law now, a party may become entangled in a patent infringement dispute without directly infringing the patent. This situation often affects contract manufacturers who produce parts for other entities that then use those parts to infringe.

Although there are jurisdictional differences, a verdict of contributory infringement typically involves:

Existence of Direct Infringement

There must be an underlying act of direct infringement by another party.

Material Component

The supplied component must be a significant or material part of the invention, often specifically made or adapted for use in infringement.

Lack of Non-Infringing Uses

The component must have no substantial non-infringing applications.

The case of Global-Tech Appliances, Inc. v. SEB S.A. (2011) clarified the standards for contributory patent infringement, particularly the concept of "wilful blindness". SEB, a French company, sued Global-Tech for infringing its patent on a cool-touch deep fryer. Global-Tech's subsidiary, Pentalpha Enterprises, had reverse-engineered SEB's product without realising it was patented in the United States and then sold it to companies like Sunbeam, who marketed it in the United States.

In this case, the jury awarded SEB US $4.65 million in lost profits damages against Pentalpha. After multiple appeals, the US Supreme Court upheld the damages, underscoring that a defendant may be held liable for patent infringement under "wilful blindness" if they take deliberate actions to avoid acknowledging a high probability of infringement.

This ruling has significantly impacted how companies approach product development and sales strategies, highlighting the importance of thorough patent research (part of competitive intelligence) and careful due diligence.

Contract manufacturers can be vulnerable to contributory infringement if they unthinkingly produce product for a customer without checking potential liabilities.

34

THE PATENT GRANT PROCESS

The process for securing patent rights is broadly similar worldwide, as outlined in the flow chart below.

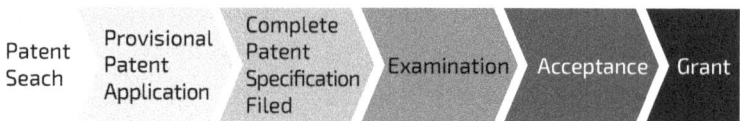

Patent Seach → Provisional Patent Application → Complete Patent Specification Filed → Examination → Acceptance → Grant

The main stages include:

Patent Searching

I consider that conducting initial competitive intelligence is essential, but unfortunately this is not a compulsory step. Not only does this act as a preliminary check, potentially avoiding "reinventing the wheel", but it can also reveal technologies that may enhance the invention. Expired patents are a particularly rich source of information.

Searching can provide insight into other market players, who could be competitors or potential collaborators. Often, the same inventors appear within a specialised field, which may be advantageous if the business is considering new hires.

Patent searching can also reveal market demand for the invention, its patentability, and any risk of infringing existing patents.

Before proceeding to manufacturing, a thorough search and analysis by an IP specialist is highly advisable. This step provides greater assurance regarding key issues, especially related to potential patent infringement.

Additionally, a formal report from a patent attorney can serve as valuable evidence in case of future infringement disputes.

The Competitive Intelligence section provides additional insights.

Patent Application

Patent applications generally follow a phased approach, allowing for the development and validation needed to turn an invention into a commercial product or process.

Provisional Patent Application

The first phase commonly involves filing a provisional patent application. This entails submitting a patent specification (see Chapter 32), which may or may not include patent claims, describing the invention as it stands and how it may develop.

Filing a provisional patent application establishes what is known as a priority date. In most countries, the earliest priority date secures the rights, making "first to file" the rule.

In some cases, patent applications for very similar inventions have been filed within days of each other, with no causal connection. A theory exists around an "invention ether", suggesting that inventors are exposed to similar factors influencing development. Thus, timing is critical; a one-day delay could mean the difference between holding a monopoly on the invention and losing those rights and being prevented from commercialising your invention.

With the greater use of AI and potentially shared training datasets, the "invention ether" is becoming more prevalent.

The timing of a patent filing considers various factors, including:

- ✓ The specific patent laws of each country
- ✓ The invention's development stage
- ✓ Likely progress of competitor developments
- ✓ When the invention will be commercialised or published
- ✓ The workload of the patent attorney.

Complete Patent Application

The second stage is filing a complete patent specification, typically within 12 months of filing a provisional patent specification. This may occur in the same country as the provisional application and/or other countries, or as part of an International (PCT) patent application (see International Applications below).

The complete patent specification often contains the contents of the entire provisional patent specification, along with additional design features, supporting data, and a full set of patent claims.

Once filed, the body of the complete specification cannot be amended except under exceptional circumstances. However, patent claims can be amended (see Examination discussion below), but only if these amendments are substantiated by the specification's content.

Examination

A country's Patent Office employs patent examiners to ensure that patent rights are awarded only to rightful claimants, ostensibly on behalf of the public. In contrast, patent attorneys are advocates for the patentee's rights, seeking maximum protection for their clients.

The interaction between patent examiners and attorneys can be intense, challenging, and costly.

The **Three Cogs Formula** approach can ease the patent examination process. Comprehensive competitive intelligence enables a patent attorney to draft a more precise specification that can forestall patent examiners' objections.

Conversely an examiner's report can also provide additional competitive intelligence, alerting a patentee to potential minefields around Freedom to Operate, competitor/collaborator activity and how crowded a particular field is.

Acceptance and Grant

Once the examiner is satisfied, the patent application is accepted and advertised as such. This initiates an opposition period (often three months, sometimes extendable), during which other parties may object. If there are no successful objections, the patent is granted, giving exclusive rights to make, sell, license, use, import, and export the claimed invention within the granting country.

In general, patents remain valid for 20 years, provided renewal fees are paid.

International Applications

Most countries are members of the Patent Cooperation Treaty (PCT). This Treaty allows for international patent applications to have a priority backdated to the original filing date if they are filed within 12 months of the initial application,

National applications may be filed directly in individual countries or through the PCT route, which enables a single application with the option to file in over 150 countries later.

Knowing the process of a patent application can guide other business decisions such as timing of research, marketing and budget allocation.

35

INVENTORSHIP AND OWNERSHIP

"No one can come and claim ownership of my work. I am the creator of it, and it lives within me."

PRINCE, AMERICAN SINGER-SONGWRITER AND MUSICIAN

Two parties are referenced in a patent application: the inventor and the applicant.

Inventorship

Inventorship is a key concept in patent law, determining who has the right to be listed as an inventor on a patent application and, subsequently, on the issued patent. While jurisdictional nuances exist, there are common principles in many countries. Notably, inventorship pertains to the claimed invention, not necessarily a product or process described in the patent specification.

The principles of inventorship include:

Conception of the invention: Inventorship is based on who conceived the invention as claimed.

Contribution to the claimed invention: An individual must have made a substantial contribution to the conception of at least one claim in the application to be listed as an inventor. Simply contributing to the project, being a project leader, or providing general guidance does not qualify one as an inventor.

Collaborative effort: If the invention results from collaboration, each contributor to the claimed invention must be listed as an inventor, regardless of whether they contributed to every claim. Noting that generative AI cannot be considered an inventor.

Omission and misjoinder: Incorrectly listing or omitting inventors can lead to invalidation or require correction of the patent.

No financial requirement: Inventorship is based solely on intellectual contribution, not financial input.

Ownership

Patent ownership refers to the legal rights held by a person or organisation in relation to a granted patent. These rights include the ability to make, use, sell, or license the patented invention, and to prevent others from doing so without permission.

IP should be thought of as any other piece of property, and ownership can be transacted through a variety of means as discussed below.

Patent Applicant

The recorded patent applicant is usually considered as the owner of the invention.

Inventor as the initial owner

In some countries, (e.g., the United States), the inventor is considered the first owner of any invention they create. If there are multiple inventors, they may be co-owners unless an agreement states otherwise.

Employer ownership

In many countries, if an invention is made by an employee in the course of their normal duties, and those duties could reasonably be expected to result in inventions, then the employer will usually own the patent.

Assignment of rights

Ownership can be transferred or assigned to another party (such as a company or individual). This must be done in writing and signed by the assignor to be legally valid. Assignments are often used in collaborations, research contracts, or when an employee starts their own venture.

As in some countries the inventor is considered first owner, then best practice involves a written patent assignment between the inventor(s) and the intended owner at the beginning of the patent process.

Inheritance

IP is considered personal property, the same as jewels, land and monetary assets. Therefore, upon death of an IP owner, ownership can be transferred to the IP owner's heirs.

Joint ownership

Patents can be owned jointly, either through co-inventorship or transfer. Each co-owner typically has the right to exploit the patent but may need consent from the other(s) to license or assign it, depending on the jurisdiction or any agreement in place.

Licensing

Ownership remains with the patent holder, but others may be granted permission to use the invention through a licence. Licences can be exclusive or non-exclusive and may carry conditions or royalties.

Disputes and clarification

Disputes about ownership can arise, especially in academic or collaborative settings. Keeping clear contracts and IP policies helps to avoid misunderstandings. Courts can also determine ownership, if necessary.

Clarify inventorship and ownership before filing a patent application to establish expectations and prevent expensive disputes when the value of the patent is realised.

36

TRADE SECRETS

"Three may keep a secret, if two of them are dead."
BENJAMIN FRANKLIN, PROLIFIC AMERICAN INVENTOR
AND BELIEVER IN OPEN INNOVATION

As an alternative to patents, trade secrets are a valuable form of intellectual property for protecting technology. However, relying on trade secrets has its own set of benefits and drawbacks. Here is a closer look at each:

Pros of Trade Secrets

No registration requirements

Unlike patents or trade marks, trade secrets do not require formal registration, saving time and costs associated with registration processes.

Immediate protection

Trade secrets are protected as soon as they are identified and reasonable steps are taken to maintain confidentiality. There is no examination or approval process, as with patents.

No time limit on protection

Trade secrets can last indefinitely, provided they remain confidential. This is a marked contrast to patents, which generally expire after a maximum of 20 years, or copyright, which also has limited terms.

Broader scope of protectable information

Trade secrets can cover a diverse range of information not eligible for other IP protections, including formulas, processes, designs, data compilations, customer lists, and business strategies.

Cost-effective

With no application fees or renewal costs, trade secrets can be more economical than securing patents or trade marks, assuming effective confidentiality measures are in place.

Protection from improper acquisition

Trade secrets prevent unauthorised use by those who acquire them through improper means, such as theft or corporate espionage, and can protect against misuse by former employees or business partners. The springboard injunctions discussed in Chapter 25 can also apply here.

Cons of Trade Secrets

No protection against independent invention

If others independently discover or reverse-engineer the information, they can use or patent it, which diminishes the value of the trade secret.

Risk of exposure

Once a trade secret is disclosed, either intentionally or through an accident (e.g., a security breach or a disloyal employee), it loses its protected status. This differs from patents or copyright, where protection persists even if the information is made public.

Limited legal recourse

The holder must prove misappropriation, and unlike registered IP, where ownership is straightforward, trade secrets require evidence of reasonable steps taken to maintain confidentiality.

Employee mobility and risk

Employees with access to trade secrets pose a risk. Even with non-disclosure agreements (NDAs) and non-compete clauses, former employees may inadvertently or intentionally disclose sensitive information, particularly in high-turnover industries.

No exclusivity for similar information

If a competitor independently develops similar processes or products, a trade secret offers no recourse, which can be a significant drawback in competitive markets.

Complex management requirements

Maintaining a trade secret demands stringent security measures, including physical, digital, and legal protocols. This can be challenging and costly, particularly for smaller firms.

Difficult valuation

Assigning value to a trade secret is complex, which can reduce its attractiveness in business transactions such as mergers or licensing. The reliance on ongoing secrecy may make potential buyers cautious.

When to Use Trade Secrets	When Not to Use Trade Secrets
Has lasting value and is difficult to reverse-engineer	Can be reverse-engineered with ease
Would not be readily discoverable by competitors without improper means	Is likely to become public knowledge or obsolete quickly
Cannot be patented or is not eligible for patent protection but still offers a competitive edge	Derives value from public disclosure
Involves customer relationships or business practices that would lose value if made public	When you have to divulge valuable details to a third party who may not be security conscious (say a manufacturer)

If choosing trade secrets over patents consider the nature of the information, the industry context, and the your capacity to maintain confidentiality.

37

OPEN SOURCE

"I think Open Source is the right thing to do the same way I believe science is better than alchemy."
LINUS TORVALDS, FINNISH SOFTWARE ENGINEER AND CREATOR OF LINUX

Many patent attorneys are nervous of open-source models and the Pandora's box that they open. Yet, surprisingly, leveraging open-source principles strategically can eventually create a competitive advantage. By open-sourcing your technology, you can accelerate the adoption of the foundational technology.

Then, if you develop an improvement on the base technology, you can choose to patent it, securing a monopoly on the best version of the technology now widely used in the market.

The competitive advantage gained through this approach can be substantial, depending on:

✓ The breadth of the customer base adopting the original open-sourced technology

✓ What others are willing to pay for the enhanced version.

However, using others' open-source technology (such as software) can come with conditions which must be considered in the context of how you want to use the open-source technology.

The principle of "copyleft" is often applied, an arrangement whereby software or artistic work may be used, modified, and distributed freely on condition that anything derived from it is bound by the same conditions.

The table below compares some more common conditional uses.

Licence	Copyleft	Attribution	Proprietary Software	Patent Grant	Source Code Disclosure	Trade Mark Use
MIT	No	Yes	Yes	No	No	No
Apache 2.0	No	Yes	Yes	Yes	No	No
GPL v3	Yes	Yes	Yes	Yes	Yes	No
BSD 3-Clause	No	Yes	Yes	No	No	No
AGPL v3	Yes	Yes	No	Yes	Yes	No
EPL	Yes	Yes	Yes	Yes	Yes	No

Next is the fourth and final Quarter of Competitive Edge: Design.

QUARTER 4
DESIGN AND INDUSTRIAL COPYRIGHT

"The straight line belongs to men, the curved one to God."
ANTONI GAUDI, SPANISH ARCHITECT AND DESIGNER

Often overlooked, and in the shadow of the flashiness of a cool brand or the wow factor of a new technology, the fourth competitive edge Quarter—design—still merits consideration.

Design frequently influences purchasing decisions; it is often how a product looks and feels that seals the deal. An effective design can elevate an ordinary item to a premium level; a playful design can create charm in kitsch products.

Conversely, a poor design can send a functional product straight to the discount aisle.

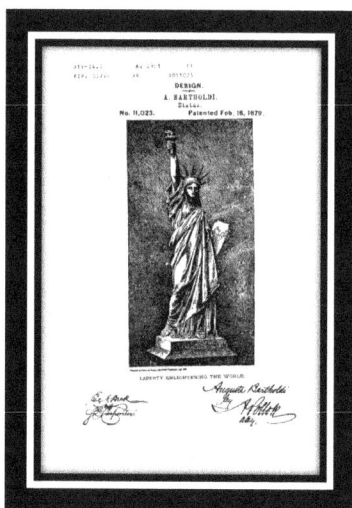

I was fortunate to be able to travel nationwide with innovation and design experts, conducting workshops that brought our three disciplines together. It was enlightening to witness the power of diverse collaborative thinking in business and beyond.

In essence, design thinking is a human-centred approach to solving problems through empathy, experimentation, and iteration. This approach can be applied to all four competitive edge Quarters, but it has a transformative impact when focused on design.

Many who appreciate design aesthetics deplore that, often, product designers do not take time to elevate their products.

While some jurisdictions protect industrial designs as unregistered copyrights, most countries offer protection only through design registration ("design patents" in the United States). Design registrations safeguard a product's visual elements, including shape, pattern, and configuration. This protection is crucial in sectors where aesthetics sway consumers, such as fashion, electronics, and household items.

Frankly, from an intellectual property perspective, the laws and the approach by various parties take to the protection of design elements is muddled. Working out the correct approach often will require the services of a professional in this area. That said, the following discussion should give some clear pointers as to the path to take.

But first it helps to gain an appreciation of what well-known products have been registered as designs.

D19-34.5   AU 2901   EX
FIP: 05/96   XR   D011023

DESIGN.
A. BARTHOLDI.
Statue.

No. 11,023.   Patented Feb. 18, 1879.

Copyright by HENRY DE PEYSTER and AUGUSTE BARTHOLDI, Aug., 1876.

LIBERTY ENLIGHTENING THE WORLD.

Auguste Bartholdi

(signatures)

38 NOTABLE DESIGNS

Here are some iconic registered designs along with the figures from the actual design registrations.

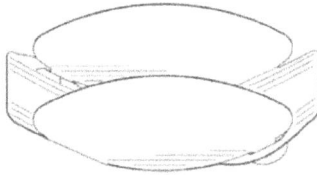

Burger Fuel® Doofer

A great New Zealand invention, which this company advertises as "a world first, magic piece of burger holding, folding cardboard genius that reduces the juices to keep your outfits looking sexxxaaaaay!"

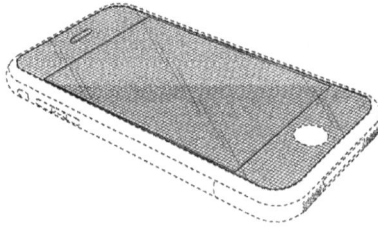

iPhone 4

Released in 2010, the iPhone 4 featured a sleek, minimalist design with a glass front and back, and a stainless-steel frame. Steve Jobs' design approach centered on simplicity, user-friendliness, and a holistic view of design as integral to the product itself, not just an aesthetic layer. He believed in making products intuitive and easy to use, focusing on the user experience and connecting technology with everyday life.

Eames Wooden Lounge Chair

The Eames Lounge Chair was named the greatest design of the 20th century by Time magazine. It used two pieces of plywood combined with a plywood spine, and the curved shape mimicked the human leg. Note that design registrations do not specify materials and only cover shape (in this instance) or pattern.

Tesla Steering wheel

This is a sleek yet distinctive design. Unusually, the Tesla logo can be seen (just) on the design drawings, as normally this extraneous material is omitted when applying for design protection.

NutriBullet® Blender

The compact, bullet-shaped design of the NutriBullet has both aesthetic and practical considerations. It has a small bench footprint and the feet on the "cup" enable it to be inverted and stand-alone.

Red Bull Energy Drink Can

The sleek, slim design of the Red Bull can, combined with its distinctive blue and silver colour scheme (colours are not part of the US design patent), has become synonymous with energy drinks. This illustrates how commodity (energy drinks) producers try to differentiate themselves through packaging design.

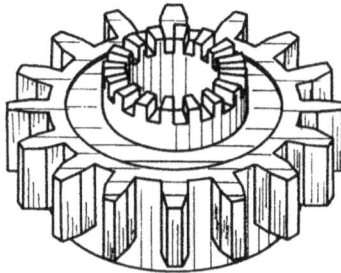

Lego Cog

The cog is just one of hundreds of Lego components which are registered as designs. This approach of protecting multiple individual components is sometimes known as "picket fencing", as it puts up many small barriers to a competitor, making it difficult for them to navigate around.

GoPro Camera

The original compact and rugged design of the GoPro has made it the go-to camera for action enthusiasts. Dozens of equally functional and yet aesthetic GoPro features have been registered since this design.

Louis Vuitton Bag

This handbag is the subject of just one of Louis Vuitton's approximately 12,000 patents and design registrations, illustrating one way this serious design company invests heavily in protecting its competitive edge.

Bialetti Coffee Pot

This is a design variant on Bialetti's 90-year-old Moka Express coffee maker. As design registrations have a limited life, it is important to keep designing and protecting the latest designs.

39

FUNCTIONAL VS.
AESTHETIC DESIGNS

Design registrations do not just cover decorative or quirky products; they can also protect practical items.

The rules for registering design elements vary between countries, particularly in how they treat functional versus aesthetic aspects of a design. Your professional advisor can guide you (as the rules keep changing), but the following gives an appreciation of the differences across a few countries.

Australia: does not require a design to be aesthetically pleasing or "eye-appealing" to be registrable. A design is registrable if it is new and distinctive when compared to prior art, regardless of its functional aspects.

China: Designs with primarily functional features are accepted if they include any unique visual element that is non-functional. The design must not serve solely a functional purpose.

European Union (Community Design Regulation): Protects only designs with an aesthetic or decorative quality. Purely functional designs without visual appeal are ineligible.

India: Registration emphasises the need for aesthetic elements, so purely functional designs do not qualify.

Japan: Purely functional designs can be registered, especially if they feature distinct shapes. However, even a slight aesthetic component can strengthen the case for registration.

New Zealand: The design can be functional but must have an aesthetic element and not be wholly dictated by function.

South Korea: Functional designs can be registered if they exhibit unique shapes or forms, even without a strong aesthetic component.

United Kingdom: Designs must have aesthetic elements; purely functional designs are excluded unless they feature some form of embellishment.

United States: Functional designs may qualify for utility patents (what the United States calls patents for technical features), but design patents (known as design registrations elsewhere) require at least a minimal ornamental aspect.

While jurisdictions like Australia, China, Japan, and South Korea are more accommodating of functional designs with unique shapes, regions such as the EU, UK, New Zealand and the United States mandate a clear aesthetic component.

Understanding what degree of aesthetics is required is crucial for successfully registering designs internationally.

40

DESIGN SCOPE

When preparing a design application, what is included in a design drawing (or left out) can be pivotal to the scope of rights achieved by the registration. While patents outline distinctions between inventions and prior art in words, design registrations are defined visually, with minimal text.

And, unlike patent claims carefully crafted by a patent attorney, design drawings are usually supplied by the designer. This can lead to inadequate rights obtained unless guidance is provided by a specialist in design registrations.

In general, the more detail provided in a design drawing the narrower the protection. It is possible to avoid infringing a design registration by omitting some details in a design registration. Therefore, be careful to include only essential design details you wish to protect.

Also consider what are the generic elements in your design. For example, an organisation may develop a suite of products with common design elements—say, gardening tools with distinctive handles. The design registrations should be in relation to the handles only and disclaim the generic part of the design such as the operational ends of the tools.

Sometimes there may be dimensional differences in a product, such as the shaft length of a gardening tool. It is possible to provide drawings that indicate that a non-essential element can have variable length.

Another factor that can affect the scope of rights is prior art. Most IP rights hinge on novelty—the differences between new intellectual property and what is already available. Thus, a valid design registration requires that the design hasn't been publicly disclosed before application. While often the effect of prior art is weaned out when patent claims are examined, this is not usually achievable in the design examination process.

Where numerous similar designs exist, determining the exact scope of a registration can be challenging. To clarify the scope of a design registration's protection, I have employed a visual evolutionary approach.

Starting with research on similar designs, I place the registered design centrally, add the alleged infringing design beside it, and then arrange comparable designs to show an evolutionary path of distinct design features. Although subjective, this arrangement often clarifies whether an "infringing" design too closely resembles the protected one.

Think about the scope of protection you want and what is already in the public domain. Then craft the design drawings accordingly.

41

A MULTI-PRONGED APPROACH WITH DESIGNS

IP rights should never be viewed in isolation.

When managing IP portfolios, I have a product-based approach with the portfolio organised to show the multiplicity of protection strategies that apply to a single product.

Compared to patents, design registrations are faster and more affordable to secure. However, as their scope is limited to appearance alone, design registrations lack the broader functional coverage offered by patents.

A tactic can be to file design applications that deter would-be competitors from taking the path of least resistance and closely copying the shape of a product.

Thwarted by the design registration, the competitor may then try to design around the design registration by having a differently shaped product which may still be competitive as it is functionally similar.

Hopefully by that time, a patent has been granted for those functional features, again stalling the competitor.

And as discussed previously, a truly iconic design can eventually become a brand in its own right and acquire additional rights through reputation and trade mark registration.

A design registration in combination with other IP rights gives synergistically stronger protection.

42

THE DESIGN REGISTRATION PROCESS

A generic design registration process is shown below.

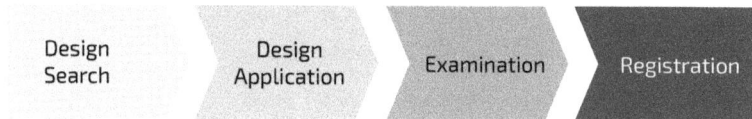

| Design Search | Design Application | Examination | Registration |

This section outlines the key stages in securing registered designs (or design patents) noting where it diverges from the patent process.

Design Searching

Before even working on a new design, it is helpful to carry out a design search. As with patents, this forms part of good competitive intelligence. It helps to identify whether similar designs already exist and may indicate whether a design is eligible for protection.

Design searching can:

- ✓ Reduce the risk of unintentional infringement—but note that this is less likely with designs compared with patents
- ✓ Provide insight into competitor activity or trends—which can influence product development and design strategy
- ✓ Reveal expired designs that may be freely used—which can be a valuable and/or fraught decision to take—noting that some distinctive designs can acquire brand reputation beyond the life of a design registration.

While businesses can undertake initial searches themselves via national or international design databases (e.g. EUIPO, WIPO Global Design Database), a comprehensive search by an IP professional is strongly advised prior to significant investment in the design process. This reduces the risk of infringement disputes and strengthens the case for protection.

Design Application

Design applications are usually more straightforward than patent applications. The focus is on the visual appearance of a product rather than its technical features or function.

An application typically includes:

✓ High-quality representations or photographs of the design

✓ A description (where required) identifying the product to which the design is applied

✓ A statement of novelty (optional in some jurisdictions)

✓ Details of the applicant and designer(s).

Many countries allow applicants to defer publication of the design to preserve confidentiality while products are prepared for launch or patent applications are being prepared—an option that can be strategically useful.

Design Drawings

Design drawings need to meet certain criteria as below.

Clear representations: The representations should be clear, crisp, and accurately depict the design's features.

Multiple views: You need to show the design from multiple angles to allow a clear understanding of its appearance from all sides.

Labelling: Each view should be labelled with the specific view shown (e.g., "Front View," "Left Side View," "Perspective View").

Format: You can use black and white photographs or line drawings.

Background: The representations should only show the product on a blank background.

No extraneous matter: Avoid including dimensions, descriptive text, or other unnecessary elements in the images.

File format: Upload images as ".jpg" or ".gif" files.

Set of articles: If the design is for a set of articles, the representations should illustrate the design applied to every article of the set.

However, as discussed in the Design Scope chapter 40, the content of the drawings needs to be carefully considered.

International Design Applications

Like the international PCT treaty for patents, there is an equivalent one for designs. International design registration can be sought through the Hague Agreement Concerning the International Registration of Industrial Designs. This WIPO-administered treaty enables applicants to file a single application that can cover multiple member countries.

Key points:

✓ A Hague application may be filed directly through WIPO, or via your national IP office if allowed.

✓ The application is examined according to the laws of each designated country.

✓ Not all countries are members (e.g., New Zealand is not), so separate national filings may still be needed in some cases.

Design Ownership and Authorship

As with patents, it is important to distinguish between the designer (who creates the design—similar to patent inventor) and the applicant (who seeks to own the right).

✓ In some countries, rights initially vest in the designer unless assigned.

✓ In others, such as the UK, designs created by employees in the course of employment automatically belong to the employer.

Best practice is to clarify ownership by having a written design assignment or employment agreement in place before filing.

Examination

Design examination is generally limited in scope compared to patents. Some countries (such as the UK and EU) perform only a formalities check to ensure that the design:

✓ Qualifies as a design (i.e. relates to appearance)

✓ Is new and has individual character (novelty and distinctiveness)

✓ Meets filing requirements (e.g., image clarity, fee payment).

Other countries (such as China or the US) may conduct a substantive examination, which can lead to objections or refusals. Responses will be required to overcome these and obtain registration.

Registration and Publication

If the application passes examination, the design is registered and published (unless deferred). Registration confers the exclusive right to use the design in commerce and to stop others from doing so without permission.

Registered design rights typically cover:

✓ Making, offering, or putting on the market any product incorporating the design

✓ Importing, exporting, or using such products.

In many jurisdictions, the initial term is five years from the filing date, renewable in five-year blocks with there being variable maximum terms in different jurisdictions.

Registered designs are a powerful tool to prevent copycat products. However, enforcement depends on how well the design has been captured in the registration, and whether it can be shown to be infringed.

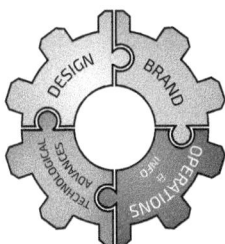

COMPETITIVE EDGE RECAP

By now I hope that you have a good appreciation of the first cog in the Hidden Mechanics and have a greater understanding of intellectual property and its relevance in a business context.

We have explored the four Quarters of:

Brand – the most valuable IP, often encapsulated in trade mark registrations and supported by good systems

Operations and information – the backbone of any business; tricky to protect formally, relying upon relationships and good internal practices

Technological advances – cool inventions which are covered by patents and trade secrets, and are sometimes open-sourced

Design – aesthetic creations whether in stylistic shape or patterns and afforded protection through copyright or design registrations.

Competitive intelligence the second cog is expanded upon in the next section and should arm you with insights that will optimise your competitive advantage.

SECTION 2

THE 2ND COG
COMPETITIVE INTELLIGENCE

"It is a capital mistake to theorise before one has data. Insensibly one begins to twist facts to suit theories, instead of theories to suit facts."

SHERLOCK HOLMES, DETECTIVE, POSSIBLY FICTIONAL

Competitive Intelligence – Overview

This section focusses on attaining fuller competitive intelligence through knowledge of IP. We'll explore various types of research along with useful tips and lessons learnt the hard way. You'll learn the foundations for the next steps of understanding your competitive edge and how to leverage it.

It can be easy to assume that before embarking on a potentially expensive project, a business or research organisation has done their homework. Unfortunately, this is often not the case.

One valuable lesson I learned early in my career was that not everyone views their innovations through the same lens as a patent attorney. The "Early Lesson Learnt" story is one such exemplar. Unfortunately, it's a story that has been echoed in various forms throughout my career.

When science researchers conduct comprehensive scientific literature reviews, they can overlook potentially more relevant information, such as commercial applications of the research they are working on. Marketers may develop a new brand but not realise that it is dangerously close to what is already protected in a potential market.

When patent attorneys conduct their own research to deepen their understanding of a particular technology, they sometimes uncover highly pertinent information that not only undermines the patentability of the research outcomes but, sadly, also undermines the hopes and dreams of their clients. From a commercial perspective, you hope that this occurs before further investment is made into patents and commercialisation. From a personal perspective, you just wish clients had done their homework before they and you got personally invested in the next shiny idea.

It is equally disappointing to have to rescue a client who invested heavily in manufacturing, packaging, marketing, and selling, only to discover they infringed trade mark rights and must recall all their goods.

It is fair to say that competitive intelligence is often not invested in sufficiently before a new project is undertaken or a new market entered. And conventional market validation only goes part way there.

Competitive intelligence also involves understanding a business's position in the market relative to others. When deeply involved in the day-to-day operations, it can require significant effort and self-awareness for a business owner to step back and view their enterprise through an external lens.

As such, a competitive intelligence exercise can be applied not only to a business's markets and competitors but also to the business itself. It's important to remember that potential competitors and collaborators could be conducting similar analyses. This approach helps identify weaknesses to address along with strengths to leverage.

Additionally, when seeking investment from external parties, the ability to critically assess your own business can instil greater confidence in potential investors.

An investment in sound competitive intelligence builds stronger strategies, ensures better protection, increases investor confidence, avoids failures and maximises opportunities.

Early lesson learnt

Pre-Google, I worked with an organisation that had dedicated years and significant resources to developing what they believed to be the perfect horticultural tool. When their patent applications were examined, a highly relevant US patent was discovered for a similar, and arguably superior, product that threatened to derail the entire project.

Feeling disheartened, I decided to deliver the news to the research team in person. To my surprise, I was met with uncharacteristic nonchalance. The researchers revealed that they were already aware of the other product and suspected it was, in fact, the inspiration for their own project from the outset!

This was one of the rare occasions when words failed me...

43

MARKET VALIDATION

"I dream of a better tomorrow, where chickens can cross the road and not be questioned about their motives."

RALPH WALDO EMERSON, AMERICAN ESSAYIST

Market validation is a valuable component of competitive intelligence, and I recommend that this is always undertaken, either by a business itself or professional market researchers.

Standard market validation generally covers the following:

Category	Details
Target Customer Profile	Demographics (age, gender, income, education, etc.); psychographics (lifestyle, values, motivations); behavioural patterns (buying habits, media consumption, brand loyalty); needs, pain points, and desires
Problem–Solution Fit	Is the problem significant enough to warrant a solution? Does the proposed product or service meaningfully address the need? Are there alternatives, and how does this compare?
Market Size and Segmentation	Total Addressable Market (TAM); Serviceable Available Market (SAM); Serviceable Obtainable Market (SOM); Geographic, demographic, or industry segmentation
Competitive Landscape	Key competitors and substitutes; market positioning of competitors; SWOT analysis (Strengths, Weaknesses, Opportunities, Threats); barriers to entry

Customer Willingness to Pay	Price sensitivity testing; expected value versus cost; buying frequency and purchasing authority
Channel Validation	Preferred sales/distribution channels; online vs offline preferences; key influencers or decision-makers in the purchase journey
Regulatory and Compliance Factors	Industry-specific regulations; local/ international compliance hurdles; certifications or standards that may affect market entry
Early Adopter Feedback	Interviews or surveys with potential early users; interest in prototypes or MVPs; Net Promoter Score (NPS) or equivalent satisfaction indicators
Purchase Drivers and Inhibitors	What compels a customer to buy? What concerns or objections might block a sale? Importance of trust signals (e.g., endorsements, reviews)
Go-to-Market Strategy Insights	Marketing channels and message testing; partnerships and influencers; timing and seasonality of demand

As impressive and useful as all this information can be, it provides only part of the picture!

Even when looking at the competitive landscape category, (which includes barriers to entry), intellectual property is not considered. This is almost negligent, considering that IP accounts for over 90% of the value of a business—yours and your competitors'.

Additional IP searching over standard market validation can reveal whether a business has Freedom to Operate in a market, whether its competitive edges are sustainable, and if they could be leveraged in negotiations with potential competitors/collaborators. But before this is done, some thought is needed as what insights you wish to gain.

44

SEARCHING WITH PURPOSE

"Behind every piece of bad content is an executive who asked for it."

MICHAEL BRENNER, CEO OF MARKETING INSIDER GROUP

IP searching is often conducted without clear intent or a plan for how to action the results.

For example, some investor organisations (governmental and commercial) have IP searching purely as a "tick-the-box", due-diligence criterion before committing funds to a project without:

- ✓ Understanding the reason to search
- ✓ Considering whether the search criteria was adequate
- ✓ Looking at the actual search results
- ✓ Understanding the outcome.

In addition, searchers are generally provided with search criteria without context. While the subsequent search results may appear impressive, their relevance to the strategic goals is often not apparent.

Intangible asset strategies help by delving into the business considerations around a project and then pull out what competitive intelligence is required and its relevance.

A dataset obtained through searching can be analysed through different lenses to extract the needed information. A single search can potentially provide all the necessary insights.

And, with the use of AI, large datasets can not only be built but also be sliced and diced with relative ease.

Back in the day, we did not have these amazing tools…

Back in the Day...

"Once a new technology rolls over you, if you are not part of the steamroller, you're part of the road."
STEWART BRAND, CO-FOUNDER, WHOLE EARTH CATALOG

I could not resist throwing in a bit of nostalgia.

The ability to conduct research has grown exponentially since I began my career in intellectual property in 1987. Initially, our focus was on IP searches within the constraints of the time. We were primarily concerned with determining whether our clients were likely to infringe on someone else's IP rights, whether an invention was patentable, or if a trade mark was registrable. The broader concept of competitive intelligence didn't even cross our minds—we were simply not that sophisticated.

At that time, New Zealand operated under what was known as "local novelty" with respect to patentability. This meant that only information publicly available within New Zealand could be used to prevent something from being patented. In theory, you could patent something that was known overseas but not locally. This led to a somewhat limited enterprise, where we would privately order US Patent Office journals to see if there was anything our clients could potentially patent in New Zealand.

Our original office in Hamilton, New Zealand, was among the first businesses to have a fax machine in that city. Such a technological advancement in communications!

Back then, we would fax a specialist searching organisation based in Lower Hutt, near the New Zealand Patent Office (now called IPONZ). The searchers would physically

travel to the Patent Office and (believe it or not) flick through cards in a filing cabinet, where patent abstracts with patent drawings, or trade marks and their goods and services descriptions, were glued onto index cards. The relevant information was then photocopied, typed up into a report, and sent via snail mail…

Prior to the fax, our only long-distance communication was via standard postal services, phone calls and a Telex machine.

Telex machines (unlike faxes) could only send text messages, and very slowly with the message being printed on paper. This did not allow the transmission of patent and design drawings, nor trade mark logos.

As IP rights often have date-critical actions associated with them, the limitations of older communications technology contributed to the lapsing of many rights. We could not file applications, make submissions, or pay fees online. Instead, we relied upon "timely" postal services. For example, a snowstorm that held up a courier van caused the lapsing of design rights—and exposed a weakness in the NZ Designs Act, which didn't permit restoration of a design registration in those circumstances.

The advent of the internet revolutionised everything, although in the early days we were slowly dialling into CompuServe via a noisy modem, around the same time we finally ditched our Telex machine.

Roll on to the modern day…

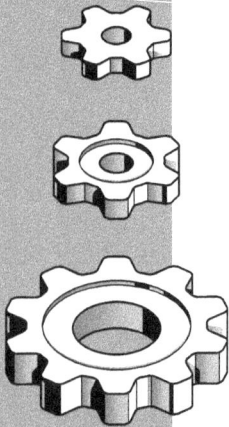

45

THE NOT-SO-SECRET SOURCES

"You can't be a real spy and have everybody in the world know who you are and what your drink is."
ROGER MOORE, JAMES BOND ACTOR

Competitive intelligence can be gathered from various sources more sophisticated than index cards, each of which can provide a different perspective.

Real-World Investigations

The world's interactions have been dramatically transformed by technology, globalisation, and a pandemic. However, face-to-face conversations, bricks-and-mortar retail, and the mood of a crowd are still relevant. Real-world research remains a powerful tool.

Engaging with fellow professionals and academics in the workplace and at events such as conferences can be incredibly valuable, not only for building collegial relationships but also for gathering crucial information that may not be available online.

Speaking euphemistically, alcohol can be the lubricant that eases information transfer.

Unfortunately, many academics unintentionally give away their valuable intellectual property without realising its true potential. For example, student posters and papers at a conference can undermine the patentability of ideas (with some exceptions) and inadvertently share clever thinking with parties who may not use the research as originally or altruistically intended.

Trade Shows

Trade shows and industry events are excellent venues for showcasing innovation and gathering competitive intelligence.

A prime example is New Zealand's iconic event, the National Fieldays, the largest agritech event in the Southern Hemisphere. On average, the

Fieldays accounts for over 60% of the exhibitors' annual sales. The lead-up to Fieldays week was always the busiest time of the year for our smaller firm, as originally the bulk of our clients were in the agriculture industry. Many of them were also exhibitors, and we scrambled to file patent and trade mark applications before our clients ended up exposing their innovations to over 100,000 attendees.

The National Fieldays has long been a hotbed of intrigue, with exhibitors scouting each other's innovations on display and even identifying potential IP infringements.

Surveys

Old-fashioned polling and market research can also be valuable sources of competitive intelligence, as discussed under Market Validation. However, care must be taken to ensure that researching the competitive landscape does not inadvertently place an invention in the public domain or inspire others to work on a similar idea. When conducting general market research, it is wise to frame questions around identifying problems rather than suggesting solutions.

For example, I have a black hole in my laundry into which numerous socks (usually one of a pair) disappears. I may have a solution to this! A survey that asks "What issues do you have when doing laundry?" is better than asking, "Would you buy socks that can button together when being washed?" *The latter giving away my cunning idea.*

Online

Online resources provide information at the blink of an eye. These resources include the ubiquitous Google, government IP databases (such as USPTO, IPONZ), PatSeq Finder (for DNA sequences), lens.org (for IP trends), subscription services, Google Patents (which is different to standard Google), private sites (e.g., Trade Mark Elite), and many more, along with AI in its various forms.

As with real-world research, there are risks. Many free online search platforms cannot guarantee the security of inputted information, which may end up being included in the datasets used to train AI. This could lead to public disclosure, rendering an invention unpatentable, unable to be commercialised, or providing competitors with clues about what others are working on.

Specialist IP searching firms, including patent attorney firms, have subscriptions to various commercial databases (such as Derwent) and possess significant experience in not only searching but also interpreting results and presenting them to clients in a readily understandable format.

Deciding whether to conduct searches in-house or to use a professional depends on internal resources such as time, budget, and in-house expertise.

For many reasons, I prefer organisations to conduct their own in-house searching, if they can. The insights gained by "doing the work" as opposed to reading someone else's search results can be significant.

Following a technological lead down the searching rabbit hole can spark new and potentially valuable ideas. And checking out competitors' trade mark registrations can guide the marketing team as to what styles and marks to avoid, so an organisation can have a more distinctive presence in the market.

If conducting in-house searching, then make sure that your searchers have some training in this area and at least follow the basic guidelines below.

More than Words

Selecting the right keywords when conducting searches is essential. Relevant information can easily be overlooked if the incorrect synonym (or none at all) is used.

For example, if you are wanting to research waterproof footwear, then you may wish to include the following synonyms: gumboots, Wellingtons (Wellies down under), galoshes, rubber boots and rain boots.

It's also important to consider cultural and jurisdictional variations. Continuing the theme, "jandals", "thongs", and "flip-flops" all refer to the same type of footwear.

All patents are categorised using IPC codes (International Patent Classification), which professional searchers employ to enhance their keyword searches. Amateur searchers often overlook this useful tool. And they also do not appreciate the additional insights that can be gained by cross-referencing the various databases – particularly useful when rights may only be published in some countries – but not others.

When searching for trade marks, it is also necessary to account for pho-netic variations. For example, "Phred" and "Fred" might not be pleased to coexist on the market.

Image searching should be taken into consideration for both trade marks and design rights.

For DNA sequence searches, it's advisable to keep the sequence as con-cise as possible.

Conduct your initial research as broadly as possible, taking care not to inadvertently disclose sensitive commercial information. When you have narrowed down your options, then engage an IP searching profes-sional who will not only have access to more results but will also be able to interpret their relevance to your plans.

Side Story

Panic at the trade show

While at an Agricultural Fieldays event, one of my clients ran up to me shouting "Kate, Kate! One of our competitors says that our new product is infringing their copyright!"

Fortunately, I knew the following:

✓ My client was an innovative market leader and unlikely to copy another's design.

✓ My client kept good records of their design evolution.

✓ To infringe copyright, my client would have to have copied the competitor's product—not just independently designed something similar.

So, I calmly suggested that we look at my client's lab books to find evidence of their independent design process—and knock the infringement allegations on their head.

Fast forward to our stunned expressions when opening the lab books to find...

A picture of the competitor's product as the genesis of their design!

Lessons learnt included providing refresher courses on clean room design techniques and what not to record.

46

IP SEARCHING CATEGORIES

Here are some useful pieces of competitive intelligence that can be obtained through general market research and more specialised IP searching.

Competitive Landscape

This type of search provides a broad overview of where a product or service fits within the market relative to similar offerings, likely competitors, collaborators, and customers. While there can be crossovers with market validation, various IP databases are explored which give additional insights.

I recommend conducting this type of search in-house as a preliminary step to gauge the viability of a new venture in the marketplace.

Prior Art (Novelty)

As mentioned previously, "prior art" is a term used in patent law to refer to previously known material. This material can include written publications, physical demonstrations, online presence, and working the invention for commercial gain.

To recap, in general (with some exceptions), patents are valid only if:

- ✓ The invention they cover is novel; that is, it has features not previously known anywhere in the world before the patent application was filed
- ✓ The invention is considered inventive, which is a more subjective criterion.

Searching to uncover relevant prior art can be valuable to assess the competitive edge an invention may have over prior art. To do this, consider whether:

✓ There is a difference between the existing prior art and the new invention (novelty), and if

✓ The feature that creates this difference offers a commercial advantage (an indication of inventiveness).

If both conditions are met, then that feature is potentially patentable and worth patenting.

NOTE: Patentability criteria is discussed further in Chapter 27.

Stopping Competitor Rights

Another use of prior art searching is to gather material that can be used to block competitors' rights. Relevant material concerning competitors' inventions (e.g., a journal article, an archived PhD dissertation, an online publication, or an earlier patent specification) can undermine their patents – if they were published before the competitors patent application.

Sometimes, a patent examiner may not have conducted a sufficiently thorough search to challenge a patent application. For instance, the US Patent Office previously did not search Japanese patents before granting a patent. Therefore, discovering a relevant Japanese patent could invalidate an approved US patent.

More strategically, the threat of rights invalidation can be used to leverage deals. For the price of keeping quiet about potentially damaging prior art they had found, a competitor can be offered a royalty-free patent licence instead. Touting that there is a licence (without referencing that is essentially "free") can give the illusion that the patent rights were considered strong enough to engender a deal.

Determining whether others' rights could be invalidated is best left to professionals, as discussed in the next section on Freedom to Operate.

Side Story

Beating the Drums

TomTom GPS navigation and mapping company have used novelty searching tactics successfully. I was fortunate to hear directly about this from Peter Spours, their former chief intellectual property officer, when he spoke at the 2014 IPBC conference in Amsterdam.

At that time, Peter was candid about how TomTom used the results of their IP searching to gain significant commercial advantages. In particular, they used searching on non Western patents to stop competitor rights.

TomTom was generating $1.4 billion annually, held more than 1,400 patents and 900 trade mark registrations, and had invested almost $250 million per year (17%) in innovation.

Today, their market cap is estimated at around $1 billion—a truly impressive achievement!

Freedom to Operate (FTO)

This is perhaps the most misunderstood and misused area of IP searching.

Freedom to operate refers to the ability to proceed with a product, service, or branding without infringing on another party's intellectual property (IP) rights. These rights, (discussed in more detail in the Competitive Edge section), can include patents, trade mark registrations, design registrations, copyright, contractual obligations, and plant variety rights.

IP rights are powerful tools that often grant a monopoly to make, sell, import, export, and use the product or service to which the IP rights relate. Consequently, potentially infringing on others' IP rights and lacking the freedom to operate commercially in a desired area can be highly restrictive.

I have witnessed many ventures fail simply because FTO searches were not conducted before launch.

The penalties for infringing IP rights can be severe and should be avoided at all costs. These have been explored under each of the individual rights (patents, designs and trade marks). Non-IP barriers to entry can also be significant and are also discussed later in this book.

However, FTO searching can be risky if not accompanied by a thorough professional analysis of the rights found and whether they are infringed. FTO searching and analysis can also be costly.

Therefore, I often recommend conducting an FTO search only in the market(s) where a client intends to first operate—whether selling or manufacturing. This approach minimises costs and can serve as an effective fast-fail LEAN strategy. Decisions on whether to expand searching to other markets can be made before entering those markets, based on risk tolerance and budget.

If potential impediments to commercialisation are identified early, strategies can be developed to navigate around these obstacles.

An expensive piece of advice

The Polaroid v. Kodak patent infringement case of the 1980s resulted in an award of US$909 million from Kodak to Polaroid and exemplifies many FTO issues.

Apart from Thomas Edison, Polaroid's founder, Edwin H. Land, held more patents than any inventor. These included patents for:

- ✓ Self developing film
- ✓ Integral film unit with peel-apart prints
- ✓ Collapsible instant SLR
- ✓ Ultrasonic range-finding
- ✓ Polarising sheet—used in sunglasses and camera filters
- ✓ 3D viewing of films

and the list goes on…

Kodak sought early advice from its patent attorneys as to whether its new instant camera design would infringe Polaroid's patents. Given the green light, Kodak sold competing technology from 1976–1986.

Polaroid sued Kodak, not only for actual damages, but also treble damages for alleged wilful infringement by Kodak.

Because Kodak had sought advice (although the advice turned out to be wrong), they avoided having to pay the treble damages.

However, the true cost to Kodak was significantly more as they had to decommission their factory and recall their products from the market. Some estimated that Kodak was adversely impacted in the order of US $3 billion.

Remarkably, it appears that somehow the Kodak attorneys survived with their careers intact.

47

PRODUCT DEVELOPMENT

One of the more enjoyable aspects of my work has been collaborating closely with clients on their product development.

"White space" is a term used in academia, research, innovation strategy and product development. In summary, white space is an area of un-met or under-explored opportunity, where little or no existing solutions, products, or knowledge currently exist.

IP and market searches are brilliant in identifying white space!

Once this white space is found, research and development (R&D) and commercialisation strategies can be implemented to design new, non-infringing products. After the product is designed, its key features can be protected, and the market can be entered to address a consumer need.

Many pharmaceutical and chemical companies, such as Dow, adopt this approach, focusing their research on compounds where they have freedom to operate and can secure the most patent protection.

Brainstorming

Fast-paced IP searching can be a valuable adjunct to brainstorming sessions—whether for product design or brand development.

It can be frustrating when the results of a productive brainstorming session are hindered by not setting the right parameters from the start.

More critically, it can be financially disastrous to invest heavily in product manufacturing or a marketing campaign only to discover that the market cannot be entered due to FTO issues. Additionally, there's the reputational damage that can occur if a product has to be recalled.

Scaling a business with a weak IP position is also challenging and costly. This is what happens when choosing inappropriate trade marks

or developing unprotectable products. Moreover, it's disappointing to miss out on opportunities because the broader application of an idea was not recognised at the start.

These issues can be mitigated by involving an IP professional in the brainstorming session. That professional can assist by:

- ✓ Conducting real-time database searches to provide high-level advice on potential FTO issues
- ✓ Offering high-level advice on the protectability of the brand or product
- ✓ Contributing ideas on branding and product design
- ✓ Challenging the team to think about broader applications of the developed IP.

In essence, brainstorm to filter out less promising ideas - after they have been respectfully considered. Conduct more in-depth searching and analysis post-session to ensure due diligence.

Home-grown Success

An example of how an IP focus for competitive intelligence can work comes from a client of mine in the animal health business.

This client had very large international competitors. But they were unable to compete by developing new chemical compounds that treated the animal – known in the trade as actives. So how do you compete and build up the value of that business against that kind of competition?

In this case, we conducted monthly NZ patent and trade mark searching, and I met their formulation chemists and CEO each month to discuss the results. We then directed research into areas that were likely to lead to protection. This included designing products around the rights we had found and protected our "design-arounds". Many of these inventions involved better ways to deliver the actives.

This intensive interaction between researchers, patent attorneys and the CEO lead to IP protection becoming part of the culture of the organisation.

As a result, the company built an incredibly valuable cornucopia of intangible assets including patents, trade marks and trade secrets.

The resultant IP portfolio was part of the reason a multi-national purchased the company for a massive nine figure sum!

Interestingly the CEO mused afterwards that they had no idea of the real value of that IP!

Competitive and Beneficial Tensions

Competitive Tensions

Understanding the relative sizes, markets, IP rights, business models, and interests of competitors and/or potential collaborators can provide valuable insights for future collaborations, as we will be discussing further in the Collaboration section.

For example, in markets with only a few major players, licensing rights to one player can provide them with a significant competitive advantage over the other players.

Beneficial tensions

One of my clients provided an unusual but highly illustrative example of competitive tension. They were relatively small compared to their two main competitors, which between them dominated the world market.

The competitors were in a mature industry selling old-fashioned kitchen appliances. My client invented and patented a device that could be integrated with those appliances. Although the device was a small item compared to the whole product, it provided a significant improvement in the operation of their competitors' old technology.

Suddenly my client was in a prime position for a bidding war, as whichever business licensed my client's invention would have a significant advantage over their competitor.

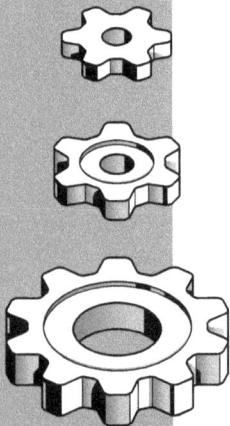

48   BARRIERS TO ENTRY – OUTSIDE TRADITIONAL IP PROTECTION

"Competition is for losers. If you want to create and capture lasting value, look to build a monopoly. Monopolies by definition have barriers to entry."

PETER THIEL, INTERNET OLIGARCH AND NEW ZEALAND CITIZEN

Competitive intelligence investigations should always cover barriers to entry that are an alternative to, or complementary to, formal IP protection. Numerous potential barriers to entry can affect a business and its competitors, which do not always involve formal IP protection like patents and trade mark registrations.

When crafting an IP strategy, I also consider:

✓ All possible barriers to entry, including general market conditions, location, historical trade within that industry, and staffing opportunities

✓ How these factors might influence business operations

✓ Where formalising or registering IP protection may be necessary if these barriers do not provide sufficient security.

Businesses should challenge their assumptions about the perceived strength of barriers to entry in a market, ensuring that decisions on where to invest time and resources are made with a full understanding of the associated risks and costs.

This is explored in greater detail in the Competitive Edge section, but first, consider the following potential barriers.

Key Personnel

Consider whether your competitor can be stymied by having the best people on your team? And who are a competitor's key personnel?

Patent searches can reveal which inventors contribute most to a competitor's innovations. Sometimes, the searches can identify inventors who are more likely to be headhunted.

Niche Markets

Competitive landscape research may identify a niche market with room for only a few players. Consider whether this is an industry that relies on a tender process for securing major contracts.

If so, mentioning relevant and exclusive IP rights in a tender document (discussed further in Chapter 21) may swing the tender your way.

Tariffs

In today's volatile world, the effect of tariffs on the viability (and thrivability) of a business is immense. Tariffs can change on a politician's whim.

Mitigate risk by having multiple export markets you can pivot to if conditions change.

Exclusive Supply

Could a key ingredient or component be in limited supply, or is access restricted to a select few? Can only a few parties manufacture a critical component? Supply constraints or exclusivity can also be leveraged into a competitive advantage.

Regulatory Approval

Industries that require regulatory approval, such as in the food, health, or veterinary sectors, often have jurisdictional standards that must be met, such as emissions or contaminant levels.

Researching regulatory restrictions or approvals (such as those from the FDA) can provide valuable information about potential barriers to market entry. It can also yield useful technical details about competitor products that have been approved.

Regulatory restrictions can also be considered when drafting a related patent specification.

Development Time

Another factor is how long it would take a well-resourced competitor to catch up. Examining when a competitor's patent applications are filed and when their corresponding products enter the market can provide a rough indication of their speed to market.

Local Knowledge

Understanding the region—even such things as weather patterns, transportation, and cultural aspects such as holidays, superstitions, and religion—may also play a role in your decision making.

COMPETITIVE INTELLIGENCE RECAP

Comprehensive investigations, including market validation, IP searching, and knowing alternative barriers to entry, understanding where tariffs apply, can give a business the competitive intelligence it needs to proceed with the next step on the business journey.

Armed with the insights gained from competitive intelligence, a business can then identify whatever intangible assets it may have that can give an edge over the competition or an edge in negotiation with a potential collaborator.

The next section explores how the third cog of collaboration if structured well can supercharge a business.

SECTION 3

THE 3RD COG
COLLABORATION

"Coming together is a beginning, staying together is progress, and working together is success."

HENRY FORD, AMERICAN INDUSTRIALIST AND BUSINESS MAGNATE

Collaboration – Overview

Collaboration—the third Cog in the Hidden Mechanics of IP— can be a challenging concept for some to embrace, particularly for those from my home country of New Zealand (see Kiwi Ingenuity Side Story). Collaboration is often shaped by cultural norms, which must be considered when introducing the idea of working with others outside an organisation in order to scale up.

No organisation operates in isolation, and achieving scale frequently depends on access to external expertise, specialised resources, and established networks. Whether through a research partnership, a manufacturing agreement, or a distribution arrangement, collaboration enables a business to expand its capabilities beyond internal boundaries.

> If you want to go fast, go alone. If you want to go far, go together.
> *AFRICAN PROVERB*

More than just gaining additional support, strategic collaboration opens up access to new markets, accelerates product development, and encourages innovation. By working alongside others, businesses can draw on complementary skills and technologies, using the strengths of their partners to build something greater than the sum of its parts. However, collaboration comes with its own set of challenges. Choosing the right partners and ensuring that intellectual property is properly positioned are essential considerations.

Without a clear strategy, there is a risk of entering into partnerships which do not align with long-term objectives or, even worse, ones that undermine a business's competitive advantage.

This section of the book is not a substitute for expertise from commercial negotiators and lawyers. Instead, it provides a high-level understanding of the role that IP can play when working with others to scale up projects.

49

HOW COLLABORATION INTEGRATES WITH THE HIDDEN MECHANICS

The **Hidden Mechanics** offers a structured framework designed to help
organisations realise the full potential
of their intangible assets. The first two
cogs of **Hidden Mechanics** play a
critical role in supporting informed
and confident decision-making when
engaging with potential partners;
that is, when working the third Cog,
Collaboration.

Competitive Edge

Effective collaboration depends
on mutual benefit. By having a clear
understanding of what differentiates
your organisation—and ensuring those
assets are well protected—you have leverage
in negotiations, regardless of your size.

Competitive Intelligence

Competitive intelligence involves activities such as conducting intellectual property searches, understanding markets, evaluating the strengths of
competitors, and confirming freedom to operate without infringing on existing rights. These insights are essential for identifying potential partners
who could offer real, strategic value.

Your proprietary technology, brand power, or operational know-how
may be useful to another party. Identifying synergies between the parties is

the start of working out what a collaboration will look like.

Recognising your own competitive edge allows you to structure agreements that maximise your advantage while reducing potential risks.

Side Story

Kiwi ingenuity, and why Kiwis don't like to play...

New Zealanders (aka Kiwis) have long been known for their fierce independence and resourcefulness, traits forged by being situated on the edge of the world with a relatively small population. Even today, New Zealand averages fewer than 20 people per square kilometre. Historically, this meant that if something needed to be done, there wasn't always an expert or ready-made solution available—so Kiwis had to figure it out themselves.

This DIY attitude, deeply embedded in the national psyche, extends from practical home projects to world-class innovations. A defining expression of this ingenuity is the Number 8 Wire mentality, named after the versatile fencing wire, that early farmers repurposed for all sorts of problem-solving. Once I even judged an agricultural "fashion" competition where many of the clothing designs included No.8 wire along with other farming paraphernalia.

This ability to "make do" with limited resources has driven a culture of practical innovation, where constraints are seen not as barriers but as challenges to overcome. It has also meant that Kiwis are less inclined than other cultures to embrace collaboration when looking to globalise their innovations.

Kiwi innovation has included the following:

Refrigerated shipping (1882) – Revolutionised global food trade, allowing New Zealand to export meat and dairy worldwide from one of the most remote countries on the planet.

Electric fencing (1930s) – Invented by Bill Gallagher Snr., this technology transformed livestock farming Gallagher Group and is known as one of New Zealand's iconic companies. Early in my career I developed with them an IP portfolio management system that I successfully replicated for other client portfolios.

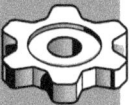

The HamiltonJet (1950s) – Developed by Sir William Hamilton, this water jet propulsion system allows boats to navigate shallow waters, widely used in rescue operations and military vessels.

Zespri kiwifruit (1997) –, New Zealand pioneered the global commercialisation of what was originally known as the "Chinese Gooseberry", and bred many popular varieties. I was fortunate enough to work in kiwifruit research and then later got to know Zespri as an IP client – helping them get plant variety rights protection for their "Gold" variety.

Bungy jumping (1980s) – Commercialised by A J Hackett, bringing adrenaline tourism to the world.

Martin Jetpack (2008) – Glenn Martin developed one of the first practical jetpacks, designed for both military and commercial use.

Rocket Lab's Electron rocket (2017) – Founded by Sir Peter Beck, Rocket Lab has pioneered cost-effective small satellite launches, making tiny New Zealand a space-faring nation.

The Electronic Distance Measurement (EDM) Device (1950s) – Created by Dr. Trevor Pearcey, this technology was a breakthrough in modern surveying.

The world's first artificial insemination of sheep (1960s) – Revolutionised the livestock breeding industry.

LanzaTech's carbon recycling (2005) – A biotech breakthrough that converts industrial emissions into biofuels and chemicals.

The Pavlova – A meringue-based dessert that has become an iconic dish in Australasia. It has been a source of cross-Tasman rivalry as the Australians have tried to claim the pavlova as their own!

Instant coffee (1890s) – David Strang from Invercargill patented one of the first instant coffee processes.

Side Story

The eggbeater (1906) – Ernest Godward invented a high-speed non-clogging eggbeater, leading to modern kitchen appliances. This was also useful for making pavlovas!

Anti-shock sheep shearing handpiece (1900s) – Improved safety and efficiency in shearing, helping New Zealand remain a leader in wool production

The Buzzy Bee toy (1940s) – Although a child's toy, it became a Kiwi cultural icon, gaining international fame when pictured alongside Prince William crawling on the lawn of New Zealand's Government House.

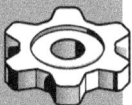

50

NOTABLE IP
COLLABORATIONS

It helps to understand what successful IP collaborations can look like, as well as appreciate the value of those collaborations. The following is a selection of globally significant partnerships.

ARM Holdings – Technology Licensing Model

Type: Patent and technology licence

Parties: ARM Holdings → Apple, Samsung, Qualcomm, Nvidia, and others

Description: ARM licenses its chip architecture and instruction sets to hundreds of tech companies for use in processors.

Estimated value: Over US$2 billion in annual licensing revenue

Significance: ARM's licensing model powers nearly all smartphones globally. It's a cornerstone example of a non-manufacturing, IP-led business.

Qualcomm – Patent Licensing in Wireless Communications

Type: Patent licensing

Parties: Qualcomm → Apple, Samsung, Huawei, and other OEMs

Description: Qualcomm holds foundational patents in 3G, 4G, and 5G technologies and licenses these to manufacturers.

Estimated value: Licensing generates ~US$6–$8 billion annually for Qualcomm

Notable dispute settled: Apple paid $US4.5 billion in a 2019 settlement to resume licensing Qualcomm's IP.

Intel and TSMC – Technology Collaboration

Type: Cross-licensing and process tech collaboration

Parties: Intel ⇔ TSMC

Description: As Intel seeks advanced manufacturing capacity, it collaborates with TSMC, which holds key process IP.

Estimated investment: Intel committed US$4 billion+ to secure manufacturing IP and capacity.

Significance: A shift in competitive dynamics where IP collaboration becomes necessary even among rivals.

GoPro + Red Bull – Co-branding and IP Sharing

Type: Co-branding partnership

Parties: GoPro ⇔ Red Bull

Description: GoPro became Red Bull's exclusive imaging partner. Red Bull received equity in GoPro in exchange for access to content and branding IP.

Estimated value: Deal value was not fully disclosed, but GoPro's market cap spiked post-announcement. Red Bull Media House IP reached new digital platforms.

Significance: Merged adventure branding IP with technology IP in a symbiotic relationship.

Nike + Apple – Co-branding + Tech IP Collaboration

Type: Co-branding and product innovation (wearables)

Parties: Nike ⇔ Apple

Description: Collaboration led to Nike+iPod and later Nike Training Club and Apple Watch Nike edition.

Estimated impact: The Nike+ ecosystem helped Apple enter fitness tracking; Apple Watch has generated US$12billion+ annual revenue.

Significance: Combined Nike's sportswear brand with Apple's tech platform using shared design and software IP.

BioNTech + Pfizer – mRNA Technology Collaboration

Type: Technology licence and joint IP development

Parties: BioNTech ⇔ Pfizer

Description: Pfizer licensed BioNTech's mRNA platform to co-develop the COVID-19 vaccine.

Estimated revenue: The Comirnaty vaccine generated US $37 billion (2021) in global sales for Pfizer.

IP elements: Joint ownership of patents and regulatory data; cross-licensing in certain markets.

Disney + Lego – Licensing Deal

Type: Copyright and design licence

Parties: Disney ⇔ Lego

Description: Lego produces themed sets based on Star Wars, Marvel, Frozen, etc., under license from Disney.

Estimated value: The Star Wars Lego line alone has generated over US$2 billion in sales since launch.

Significance: An example of long-term licensing of storytelling and character IP.

IBM – IP Licensing Programme

Type: Patent licensing programme

Parties: IBM ⇔ Global enterprises

Description: IBM has consistently earned over US$1 billion per year from licensing its technology patents across sectors including semiconductors, software, and AI.

Significance: IBM monetises R&D through a structured IP licensing strategy without always commercialising the products directly.

Dolby Laboratories – Audio Technology Licensing

Type: Patent and trade mark licence

Parties: Dolby ⇔ Electronics manufacturers (Sony, LG, Microsoft, etc.)

Description: Dolby licenses its audio technologies (e.g., Dolby Atmos, Dolby Digital) for integration in devices, cinemas, and content platforms.

Estimated revenue: Over US$1.2 billion per year from licensing

Significance: Dolby's trade marks are also licensed, meaning brand recognition is an integral part of the deal.

OpenAI + Microsoft – Exclusive IP Licensing Deal

Type: Exclusive licence to use and commercialise GPT models

🌀 **OpenAI** | ▦ Microsoft

Parties: OpenAI ⇔ Microsoft

Description: Microsoft has exclusive rights to commercial use of GPT-3 (and later versions) in Azure and other services.

Estimated value: Microsoft invested US$1 billion+, leading to co-developed IP and product launches (e.g., Copilot in Microsoft Office).

Significance: A new frontier in licensing AI model IP and embedding it in enterprise services.

The Three Cogs approach is validated by the variety and sheer scale of these real world partnerships which are based on using each others' IP.

51

WHAT DO YOU NEED?

"You can't always get what you want, but if you try, sometimes, you just might find you get what you need."

ROLLING STONES, MEGA AWESOME ROCK GODS

The previously cited collaborations provide an idea of the variety of deals that can be made.

Before seeking out a collaboration, take a step back and assess where your business could benefit from external expertise or resources. Many businesses jump into partnerships out of necessity or opportunity, without clearly defining what they need to achieve. This often leads to partnerships that don't serve long-term goals or, worse, create unnecessary complications.

R&D Support

Are you looking for research and development support—perhaps access to scientific expertise, testing facilities, or a specialised knowledge base that your team doesn't have? Universities, research institutions, and R&D-driven companies can be valuable partners when it comes to refining technology, testing new concepts, or staying ahead of industry trends.

However, academic collaborations come with their own set of challenges, particularly around ownership of intellectual property and commercialisation timelines.

Manufacturing

If manufacturing and production are your biggest hurdles, an external contract manufacturer might offer the scale and efficiency you need to grow. The question then becomes: should you go with an offshore manufacturer to keep costs down, or is maintaining local production crucial to your brand and quality standards?

Choosing the right partner means weighing cost, reliability, and quality control—while ensuring that your intellectual property is protected throughout the process.

Distribution

For businesses looking to expand their market reach, a strong distribution partner can provide access to established networks and help navigate logistical or regulatory barriers. This can be particularly useful when entering international markets, where an experienced distributor understands local business practices and can prevent costly missteps. However, distribution agreements need careful structuring: Who controls the pricing, how will your brand be represented, and what happens if the relationship ends?

Co-branding

Done right, brand collaborations can be a game-changer. If you're considering a co-branding partnership, think about whether the association will truly enhance your reputation or if there's a risk of dilution. Not all brands make good bedfellows, and a collaboration should align with your values, your audience, and your long-term positioning.

Tech Access

And then there's technology and innovation. Sometimes, the most valuable collaboration is with a company whose technology complements your own. Could integrating another company's software, platform, or product create a stronger offering? Cross-licensing agreements and technology-sharing partnerships can be highly effective, but they require careful negotiation to ensure that each party maintains control over their core intellectual property.

Regardless of the nature of the relationship with a collaborator, the relationship needs to be formalised in a written agreement with explicit clauses around intellectual property and overall expectations of the collaboration. Another situation where an experienced commercial IP lawyer should be consulted.

52

ASSESSING COMPATIBILITY

"Success in business depends more on relationships than spreadsheets."

ALAN COHEN, AMERICAN AUTHOR

In intellectual property relationships, a collaborative approach—partnering with clearly defined boundaries—is often better than an adversarial one. Litigation, while sometimes necessary, is generally a waste of time, energy, and money. It can be highly stressful and distracts business owners from focusing on more positive aspects of their commercial journey.

Not every promising collaboration will be a good fit. Before committing to a partnership, evaluate whether it aligns with your business objectives and values. Do they share your long-term vision? Will their involvement add value rather than just duplicating your capabilities? If their strengths don't complement yours, the collaboration might not bring the efficiency or innovation you're hoping for.

A partner's track record and reputation also matter. Have they successfully collaborated with others in the past, or do they have a history of failed partnerships and legal disputes? Some companies are known for being difficult partners, demanding too much control over intellectual property, or failing to honour agreements. Due diligence is critical. Check their background, ask for references, and ensure that you're entering into a relationship with a trustworthy and professional organisation.

Intellectual property negotiations can also be a major sticking point. Some companies enter partnerships with a grab-first mentality, seeking to gain as much access to IP as possible while offering little in return. It's essential to be clear about what you are—and aren't—willing to share. Are they fair in IP negotiations? Do they understand the importance of protecting each party's competitive advantage? If there are warning signs that they don't respect boundaries, it's best to walk away before any agreements are signed.

Whomever you are considering, make sure that you research them thoroughly before signing any agreement. As part of your research, ask a trusted ally for their opinion of your potential partner.

You may also wish to consider whether a collaborative partner can help with these additional issues.

Freedom to Operate

Not having Freedom to Operate (FTO) in a market can be a significant impediment, particularly if it is linked to another's powerful IP rights.

Practically, a smaller business may not have the resources or inclination to tackle potential FTO issues. But one tactic is to consider taking onboard a strategic partner who may have the negotiating power or funds to do so.

Business Models

Sometimes a smaller business may not be able to pull off an ambitious business model, but a strategic partner may be able to help.

For example, one business model is vertical integration; namely, controlling different stages along the supply chain and bringing production processes in-house. However, if the capital expenditure required for vertical integration is onerous, an alternative model could be to have control over the stages by licensing the IP to external suppliers.

Regulatory Environment

Barriers to entry such as regulatory issues may inhibit scaling of a business.

For example, a business may have good systems that meet strict regulatory requirements; say, in the manufacture of veterinary products. That business could also use or license its intangible assets to enter into other regulated environments (say, medical or food).

The business can also recognise that parties in other geographical markets could license their core systems with tweaking for a local regulatory environment, thus scaling up with minimal investment.

While all of the above are valid considerations, a less academic factor also needs to be considered. What is your "spidey sense"? To quote Oprah Winfrey "If it doesn't feel right, don't do it. That is the lesson and that lesson alone will save you a lot of grief"

53

PREPPING IP
FOR THE DEAL

"The loftier the building, the deeper must
the foundation be laid."

*THOMAS À KEMPIS, GERMAN THEOLOGIAN AND AUTHOR
OF THE IMITATION OF CHRIST*

Before entering into any collaboration, ensure your intellectual property is well structured, protected, and aligned with the partnership opportunity. Often, businesses rush into collaborations without first organising their IP assets, which can lead to unclear ownership, misaligned expectations, or lost commercial value. Proper preparation ensures that you bring something of value to the table while also safeguarding your competitive advantage.

Note that the IP you bring to a partnership is sometimes referred to as Background IP.

The first step in preparing for collaboration is conducting an internal IP audit to take stock of what you own, what you have rights to, and what might need further protection.

This includes reviewing:

Patents – Do you have any granted patents or pending applications? Are there gaps where additional filings may be needed? Do the patent claims cover the technology which will be part of the collaboration?

Trade marks – Is your brand protected in the relevant markets and goods/services classes where the collaboration will operate?

Copyright and design rights – If your business relies on creative assets or product designs, are they properly registered or documented? Copyright and design rights differ widely per country, so ensure that you have appropriate rights where you will be collaborating.

Trade secrets and confidential information – Have you put appropriate measures in place (such as confidentiality agreements and internal protocols) to protect proprietary knowledge?

Having a clear picture of your IP strengthens your negotiating position and ensures that there are no hidden vulnerabilities that could weaken the collaboration or be exploited by a potential partner. An IP strategist can help you with this aspect.

54

STRUCTURING SUCCESSFUL COLLABORATIONS

"It's never a good deal when only one party thinks it is."

MALCOLM FORBES, PUBLISHER OF FORBES MAGAZINE

By now you will have worked out what you need, what you bring to the table, and researched potential partners. You are now ready for the next stage of laying the groundwork for a formal agreement.

Collaboration can be a powerful tool for growth, but its success depends on careful planning and clear agreements. Without well-defined terms, even the most promising partnerships can run into issues around intellectual property ownership, financial expectations, or differing strategic priorities. Taking the time to structure collaborations properly ensures that both parties benefit and that potential risks are minimised from the outset.

A strong collaboration starts with a shared vision: What are both parties aiming to achieve? Defining success from the beginning helps prevent misalignment later. Both short-term and long-term objectives should be discussed openly and reflected in formal agreements. This includes outlining mutual benefits, setting realistic expectations, and ensuring that both partners understand their respective roles and responsibilities. A well-structured partnership is one where each party's contributions are valued, risks are balanced, and the agreement fosters an environment of trust and innovation.

Negotiations should aim for a win-win outcome, where both parties feel they are gaining value.

Deals structured with too much rigidity can stifle innovation, while those that are too loose can lead to misaligned expectations. The key is to remain flexible while ensuring that your interests—particularly your IP rights—are well protected. Avoid common pitfalls such as over-promising, failing to define IP ownership clearly, or agreeing to exclusivity clauses that limit your future opportunities.

55

ESSENTIAL IP LICENCE TERMS

"A verbal contract isn't worth the paper it's written on."

*SAMUEL GOLDWYN, FILM PRODUCER AND
PIONEER IN THE AMERICAN FILM INDUSTRY*

Many collaborations involve some form of intellectual property licensing. Whether it's sharing patented technology, software, or brand assets, licensing agreements must be structured carefully to ensure fairness and long-term viability. Poorly defined licensing terms can lead to disputes, loss of market control, or unintended competitive disadvantages. Key elements to consider include the following:

Ownership and Rights

Ownership of intellectual property is one of the most crucial aspects of any collaboration. Clear distinctions must be made between Background IP (existing assets that each party brings into the collaboration) and Foreground IP (new IP developed during the partnership).

Defining ownership early prevents future conflicts over commercialisation rights and revenue sharing. Additionally, freedom to operate issues (competitive intelligence again!) should be assessed. Both parties need to ensure they have the necessary rights to use and commercialise any jointly developed IP.

Scope of Licence

When licensing IP, it's important to clarify the terms of use.

Is the licence exclusive or non-exclusive?

An exclusive licence grants sole usage rights to one party, while a non-exclusive licence allows multiple licensees.

What is the geographical scope?

Does the licence apply globally (hopefully not), or is it restricted to specific regions? Earlier market research should have identified in which markets the various parties are strong.

What is the field of use?

The IP might be licensed for certain applications or industries but restricted from use in others.

These considerations help prevent conflicts and ensure that the IP is being used in a way that aligns with both parties' business strategies.

Performance and Quality Standards

Performance benchmarks should be built into the agreement to ensure that the licensee actively uses the IP rather than letting it stagnate. This could include sales targets, development milestones, or product launch deadlines.

Quality control measures are also essential—especially in franchises, manufacturing or brand licensing—to protect the integrity of the product and the business's reputation.

Audit rights may also be negotiated, allowing licensors to inspect records or facilities to ensure compliance.

Ideally, failure to meet these standards can trigger termination of the licence.

Financial Terms

A licensing agreement should clearly define the financial aspects, including:

Upfront payments – A one-time fee for access to the IP

Royalties – Ongoing payments based on revenue, sales, or usage

Minimum guarantees – A baseline revenue requirement to ensure continued value

Milestone payments – Payments triggered by specific achievements, such as regulatory approval or product launches

Structuring financial terms carefully ensures that the IP owner is fairly compensated while allowing the licensee room to succeed commercially.

Again, failure to meet these standards can trigger termination of the licence.

Litigation

Is there an obligation for any of the parties to litigate in cases of IP infringement, and if so, under what conditions?

Market and Geographic Considerations

A collaboration should open new opportunities rather than restrict them. It's important to assess how market exclusivity, licensing restrictions, or partnership terms could impact future growth.

Local regulatory compliance is another key factor, as different markets may have unique legal requirements for IP usage, health claims, manufacturing, packaging, or branding.

Share Dilution and Equity Considerations

Some collaborations involve shared business ownership. If equity is part of the arrangement, partners must agree on:

Equity stakes – What percentage of ownership each party holds.

Dilution protection – Mechanisms to prevent one party's ownership share from being diluted if new investors enter.

Exit strategies – Terms for selling or transferring ownership stakes if the partnership ends.

"Skite Rights" (Marketing and Publicity Usage)

I love the term "skite rights" and often reference the possibility of having them in IP strategies - particularly as marketing rights can be just as valuable as financial terms in a collaboration. Skite rights enable brand value to be greatly enhanced through association (even in the minor key) with a successful product, service, or organisation.

Partners should agree on how they will be publicly associated with the project and consider the following:

Attribution and recognition – Will both parties be credited equally?

Press releases and branding – How will announcements be handled, and who has final approval?

Case studies and testimonials – Can success stories be used for promotional purposes?

Clear guidelines around marketing ensure that both parties benefit from the partnership's success without disputes over public perception.

Dispute Resolution and Termination

Even well-structured collaborations can run into difficulties. It's crucial to agree in advance on how disputes will be handled.

Governing law – Which country's laws will apply?

Dispute resolution – Mediation, arbitration, or litigation?

Termination clauses – What can trigger termination (say, quality and financial performance), and what warnings/notice should be given before termination occurs? What happens if the collaboration ends? How will shared IP, assets, or obligations be handled post-termination?

By addressing these considerations upfront, partners can build a framework that supports long-term success while minimising risks and uncertainties.

Professional Guidance

I have seen too many times the pain that arises when a deal goes south and the agreements covering it have been inadequately drafted. IP licences definitely require the expertise of professionals specialising in this area.

In general, commercial lawyers are rarely exposed to reviewing or draft contracts which deal with the complexities of IP law. If you believe that your project has commercial worth, then take the time to seek out an expert to assist you.

Your expert should ideally have IP commercial law as their primary expertise—not just a side service. Preferably they are associated with a specialist IP firm so they can tap into the expertise of patent, trade mark, and copyright experts.

56

FINAL THOUGHTS

Congratulations! You have made it through to the end!

To recap the Hidden Mechanics consists of:

- Understanding what makes your innovation or business model unique (Competitive Edge)
- Conducting thorough research early on (Competitive Intelligence), and
- Knowing how to protect and leverage your intellectual property.

These three cogs should place your business in a stronger position to commercialise and capitalise on its IP, whether independently or through Collaboration.

This book has been a labour of love, drawing upon my many years and experiences in an enjoyable career. Innovation and adding value to it still excites me. I hope that this book has helped demystify IP for you and provided you with practical ways to make the most of your intangible assets.

Please reach out to me with any comments and questions.

Best wishes for your innovation journey!

Kate Wilson

ACKNOWLEDGEMENTS

"Silent gratitude isn't much use to anyone."

GERTRUDE STEIN - AMERICAN NOVELIST AND POET

This book would never have made it to the finish line without the support, encouragement, and expertise of some remarkable people.

First and foremost, my publishing coach and friend, **Dixie Carlton** of Indie Experts—thank you for prodding, cheering, and expertly guiding me through the maze to the final product. Your wisdom and persistence were just the nudge (and sometimes the shove) I needed.

To **Ammie Christensen**, whose design flair and formatting skills turned my manuscript into a beautifully structured and accessible book—your work is truly appreciated.

Thanks also to **Rosemary Hepzoden**, for her eagle eye and editorial precision, which caught the things I didn't even know I missed.

To **Kevin Roberts**, former global CEO of Saatchi & Saatchi—thank you for your perceptiveness, generosity, and infectious energy. Your ability to turn "meh" into momentum has been nothing short of transformational. I'm honoured to have your foreword in this book and your mentorship behind it.

I'm deeply grateful to my insightful beta readers—**Wayne Leech, Tony Kane,** and **Ian Boddy**—whose professional judgement and honest feedback helped shape and refine the raw manuscript. Your time and candour were invaluable.

A heartfelt thanks to the team at my old firm, **James & Wells IP Law**— my professional family and friends—what a journey we've had! I'm grateful for the camaraderie, and shared passion for the world of IP.

To my **clients**—past, present, and future—thank you for trusting me with your valuable property and your stories. You've helped shape not only this book but my career and thinking.

To the many **reviewers** who generously gave their time and discernment—your input added depth, clarity, and confidence to these pages.

Finally, to my wonderful children, **Rebecca** and **Benjamin**, thank you for your enduring support, humour, and perspective. And of course to **Allan**, my husband—your patience, encouragement, and unwavering belief in me have meant everything.

This book is for all of you.

ABOUT THE AUTHOR

Kate's journey in the business world began at the age of 27 when she became a partner in James & Wells, a budding Intellectual Property law firm that she helped transform into New Zealand's leading IP law firm. Her commercial perspective broadened quickly as she served as the liaison between James & Wells and several of New Zealand's most iconic companies, including Gallagher Group, Zespri, AgResearch, and Bomac Animal Health. Through her involvement with the internationally operating IP Business Congress, Kate gained invaluable exposure to the world's top IP advisors and strategists, further enriching her international outlook.

Kate's extensive experience in business extends beyond the realm of intellectual property. She has successfully managed her own non-IP related businesses and has held independent directorships and trustee positions on various boards. Her comprehensive business acumen was nationally recognised in 2023 when she was one of only three inductees into the NZ Hall of Fame for Women Entrepreneurs.

With university degrees in physics and chemistry, Kate is also a registered patent attorney in Australia and New Zealand, providing intellectual property strategies across a diverse range of technological fields. She was the first New Zealander to be included in IAM's top 300 International IP Strategist list, and has been recognised several times since. Her expertise has been acknowledged by the international Managing IP magazine, which named her an Expert of Experts in IP strategy, while LexisNexis honoured her with their New Zealand Client Choice Award. She is recognised as an IAM top 300 Global IP leader.

Kate's reputation as an IP educator is well established on both the international and local stages. She was invited to address Vienna's ASTP conference—an association of European Science and Technology Transfer Professionals—after her paper on brainstorming garnered attention from that prestigious organization. In New Zealand, she conducts workshops and seminars for businesses and educational institutions alike. She also initiated and edited the book The Inventor's Guide to Success.

KTPI Enterprises Ltd; www.ktpi.co.nz/welcome

Want to know more?
Connect with Kate directly?
or Leave a review?

Visit Kate's website

www.ktpi.co.nz/welcome

KTPI Enterprises Ltd

www.ingramcontent.com/pod-product-compliance
Lightning Source LLC
Chambersburg PA
CBHW040852210326
41597CB00029B/4816